The

QUICK-REFERENCE
HANDBOOK
for
SCHOOL LEADERS

A Practical Guide for Principals

A Joint Publication

CORWIN
PRESS

ONTARIO
PRINCIPALS'
COUNCIL
Exemplary Leadership
in Public Education

CORWIN PRESS
A SAGE Publications Company
Thousand Oaks, California

For information:

Corwin Press
A Sage Publications Company
2455 Teller Road
Thousand Oaks, California 91320
E-mail: order@corwinpress.com

Sage Publications Ltd.
1 Oliver's Yard
55 City Road
London EC1Y 1SP
United Kingdom

Sage Publications India Pvt. Ltd.
B-42, Panchsheel Enclave
Post Box 4109
New Delhi 110 017 India

Printed in the United States of America

Library of Congress Cataloging-in-Publication Data

The quick-reference handbook for school leaders : a practical guide for principals.
     p. cm.
Includes bibliographical references and index.
ISBN 1-4129-1458-2 (cloth) — ISBN 1-4129-1459-0 (pbk.)
    1. School principals—Handbooks, manuals, etc. 2. School management
and organization—Handbooks, manuals, etc. 3. Educational
leadership—Handbooks, manuals, etc.
LB2831.9.Q85 2005
371.2′012—dc22   2004030487

This book is printed on acid-free paper.

05   06   07   08   09   10   9   8   7   6   5   4   3   2   1

Acquisitions Editor:	Robert D. Clouse
Editorial Assistant:	Jingle Vea
Production Editor:	Tracy Alpern
Copy Editor:	Cate Huisman
Proofreader:	Scott Oney
Typesetter:	C&M Digitals (P) Ltd.
Indexer:	Pamela Van Huss
Cover Designer:	Michael Dubowe

The

QUICK-REFERENCE
HANDBOOK
for
SCHOOL LEADERS

CORWIN PRESS

The Corwin Press logo—a raven striding across an open book—represents the union of courage and learning. Corwin Press is committed to improving education for all learners by publishing books and other professional development resources for those serving the field of K–12 education. By providing practical, hands-on materials, Corwin Press continues to carry out the promise of its motto: **"Helping Educators Do Their Work Better."**

Contents

Introduction

THE QUICK-REFERENCE HANDBOOK FOR SCHOOL LEADERS: AN OVERVIEW

> *I'm the new principal . . . .*
>
> *What do I do now?*

The Quick-Reference Handbook for School Leaders is designed primarily for new principals, but it is a useful resource for all principals, vice-principals, and aspiring school administrators. The *Handbook* does not separately describe principal and vice-principal responsibilities, elementary and secondary issues, or management and leadership functions. The *Handbook* is designed to be a hands-on practical guide, wide-ranging, but not exhaustive. Please note that the *Handbook* is not legal advice. Principals and vice-principals, first and foremost, must follow their district school board's policies and procedures.

HOW TO USE THE HANDBOOK

The *Handbook* is organized so that you can quickly look up a specific topic in the index; or, browse through the table of contents to identify areas of interest. It has 28 chapters, which are listed in the table of contents. It also includes appendices, references, and a resource of checklists, routines, and other information.

Icons

The *Handbook* is divided into five sections. Each section has an icon to identify the five major areas of the book.

- Part 1 Organization and Management
- Part 2 Teaching and Learning
- Part 3 Behavior and Discipline
- Part 4 Health and Safety
- Part 5 Looking After Yourself

You will also find a series of internal icons that indicate the accompanying text is presented as:

- A Checklist
- An Overview
- Tips
- Suggestions for Getting Started
- Further Reading

Text Boxes

Three types of text boxes are used in the *Handbook*.

Chapter at a Glance Boxes

Each chapter in the *Handbook* is divided into subsections, which are also listed in the table of contents. At the beginning of every chapter, you will find an outline of the contents; an example is shown below.

At a Glance

- Before the Meeting
  Meeting Planning Checklist
  Sample Meeting Agendas
- During the Meeting
- After the Meeting

Shaded Text Boxes

Certain sections of text are highlighted in shaded text boxes, which contain information that reinforces the main message. Direct quotes are referenced at the bottom of the shaded box.

> *When a teacher makes plans to become a principal, the long-range goal is to make a difference in the lives of children.*
>
> *Teachers become principals to be instructional leaders.*
>
> —*If I Only Knew,*
> H. B. Alvy and P. Robbins, p. 37

The Voice of Experience Boxes

At the end of each chapter a quotation box, identified as The Voice of Experience, offers advice to new school administrators from experienced principals and vice-principals.

Hire well

Staffing decisions are critical.

If I could give only one piece of advice, it would be to hire well.

— *The Voice of Experience*

ADVICE FOR NEW PRINCIPALS AND VICE-PRINCIPALS

The Voice of Experience

More than 60 elementary and secondary principals and vice-principals responded to this question: "What piece of advice would you give to new administrators?" These are found at the end of each chapter in The Voice of Experience boxes described above.

Words of Wisdom: Advice From Beginning Principals

Members of the *Handbook* focus group were asked what advice they would like to pass along to new principals. The members of this focus group were first year elementary and secondary principals. See "Words of Wisdom: Advice From Beginning Principals" in Appendix F.

PART I

Organization and Management

The Role of
the Principal

At a Glance

- Duties and Responsibilities: An Overview
- The Principal's Role
- Additional Roles and Skills: A Quick Overview
    Emotional Intelligence: A Key to Effective Leadership
    Roles
    Skills
- Your Personal Vision of Your Role as Principal
- The Role of the Principal as Legally Defined
    1. *Responsibility Guidelines*
    2. *Student Safety*
    3. *Student Instruction*
    4. *Student Supervision*
    5. *Staff Supervision*
    6. *Staff Evaluation*
    7. *Staff Cooperation*
    8. *School Administration*
    9. *Access to School*
    10. *Building Maintenance*
    11. *Community*
    12. *School Advisory Group*
    13. *Reports to District*

⊚ DUTIES AND RESPONSIBILITIES: AN OVERVIEW

A principal's primary duties are to

- maintain proper order and discipline in the school;

- be in charge of, and supervise, the instruction of students; and

- organize and manage the school.

- See "The Role of the Principal as Legally Defined" in this chapter for an overview of the legal aspects of the principal's role.

- Check your state department of education Web site regularly for updates to this legal definition.

Remember: Education Web sites are where many parents get their information about education.

⊚ THE PRINCIPAL'S ROLE

Principals, under the direction of their district school boards, take a leadership role in the daily operation of a school. They provide this leadership by

- demonstrating care and commitment to academic excellence and a safe teaching and learning environment,

- holding everyone under their authority accountable for their behavior and actions, and

- communicating regularly and meaningfully with all members of their school community.

In addition, principals are responsible for the organization and management of individual schools, including the budget assigned to the school by the district. The principal is the head teacher in the school and, in addition to any teaching duties, each principal is responsible for

- determining the organization of the school and ensuring ongoing maintenance of the school buildings;

- administering the school's budget;
- admitting and placing students;
- ensuring that report cards are sent to parents;
- attending meetings, acting as a resource person at those meetings, considering recommendations, and reporting back on actions taken (or delegating those responsibilities to the vice-principal);
- developing a safe school environment with the help of parents and the community.

ADDITIONAL ROLES AND SKILLS: A QUICK OVERVIEW

The following are a few ways to describe the roles and skills required of a principal.

Emotional Intelligence: A Key to Effective Leadership

School leaders bring their values, knowledge, experience, and skill to their work each day. The understanding and appropriate application of emotional intelligence (EI) is key to effective leadership. As the challenges, demands, and complexities of the principal's role increase, this knowledge will continue to be the foundation of dynamic, successful, and effective leadership.

Emotional intelligence, unlike IQ, can be learned and enhanced. Principals and vice-principals are encouraged to read and/or take training in assessing and enhancing their emotional intelligence.

The FIVE components of emotional intelligence, as defined by Dr. Reuven Bar-On, together with their subscales, are as follows:

1. Intrapersonal

Our ability to be aware of ourselves, to understand our strengths and weaknesses, and to express our thoughts and feelings nondestructively.

- Independence
- Self-actualization
- Self-regard
- Emotional self-awareness
- Assertiveness

2. Interpersonal

Our ability to be aware of others' emotions, feelings, and needs and to be able to establish and maintain cooperative, constructive, and mutually satisfying relationships.

- Interpersonal relationships
- Social responsibility
- Empathy

3. Adaptability

Our ability to manage change, by realistically and flexibly coping with the immediate situation and effectively solving problems as they arise.

- Problem-solving
- Reality testing
- Flexibility

4. Stress Management

Our ability to manage emotions so that they work for us and not against us.

- Impulse control
- Stress tolerance

5. General Mood

Our ability to be optimistic, positive, and sufficiently self-motivated to set and pursue our goals.

- Happiness
- Optimism

SOURCE: *The EQ Edge*, S. Stein & H. Book.

Further Reading

Goleman, D. (1995) *Emotional Intelligence*

Goleman, D. (1998) *Working with Emotional Intelligence*

Stein, S., and Book, H. (2000) *The EQ Edge*

Roles

As Leader

1. Advocate

2. Articulator

3. Climate builder

4. Communicator

5. Motivator

6. Negotiator

7. Organization developer

8. Planner

9. Researcher

10. Professional leader

SOURCE: Adapted from *A New Time—A New Schoolhouse Leader,* A. J. H. Newberry, pp. 32–40.

As Manager

1. Interpersonal roles: figurehead, leader, liaison

2. Informational roles: monitor, disseminator, spokesperson

3. Decisional roles: entrepreneur, disturbance handler, resource allocator, negotiator

SOURCE: Adapted from H. Mintzberg, as quoted in *The Rookie Manager,* J. T. Straub, Figure 1-1, p. 2.

Skills

1. Interpersonal skills: leadership, sensitivity, motivation of self and others

2. Administrative skills: problem analysis, judgment, organizational ability

3. Communication skills: oral, written

4. Knowledge of self

SOURCE: *Skills for School Leaders,* National Association of Secondary School Principals, Developmental Assessment Center.

YOUR PERSONAL VISION OF YOUR ROLE AS PRINCIPAL

Consider these questions as you develop a personal vision:

- What are your duties and responsibilities under the acts and regulations, policies and procedures?

- What tasks must you carry out?
- What professional roles must you play?
- What skills do you need?
- What principle(s) will guide you?

After a couple of hectic months on the job, one new principal started to develop this personal vision statement:

First, I'll consider what's in the best interest of the students.

I'll strive to promote academic excellence and continuous school improvement.

I'm responsible for the safety and well-being of students and staff, the instruction and discipline of students, and the organization and management of the school.

My Personal Vision of My Job as a Principal

What is your personal vision of your job as a principal? Whether you are a new principal or a veteran, it's important to be able to answer this question readily, if only for yourself.

THE ROLE OF THE PRINCIPAL AS LEGALLY DEFINED

The role of principals and vice-principals is defined largely by statute and by the terms and conditions of their employment with school districts. Local district policies vary from district to district and cover a range of topics. Although relevant statutes and regulations are reasonably precise in their imposition of duties and responsibilities, the documents describing terms and conditions tend to refer vaguely to a principal's responsibility to enforce and abide by "district policy."

Set out below are various categories of principal and vice-principal responsibilities. Some duties relate to more than one category and so are reproduced in more than one section. This document is intended to provide an overview only, and does not purport to be all-encompassing.

Please note that the acts and regulations are constantly changing. Be sure to keep yourself up-to-date with all changes in statutes and the resulting revisions to district policies and procedures.

1. **Responsibility Guidelines**

   a. Maintain order and discipline in the school.

   b. Be responsible for the instruction and the discipline of students in the school.

   c. Report promptly any neglect of duty or infraction of school rules by student to parent.

2. **Student Safety**

   a. Ensure that all reasonable safety procedures are carried out in courses and activities for which the teacher is responsible.

   b. Report to the appropriate agency when there are reasonable grounds to suspect child abuse.

   c. Ensure care of students and property.

3. **Student Instruction**

   a. Supervise instruction in the school.

   b. Obtain permission to evaluate students.

   c. Arrange for home instruction for students in appropriate circumstances.

4. **Student Supervision**

   a. Ensure supervision of students when the school buildings and playgrounds are open.

b. Ensure supervision of students during the conducting of any school activity.

c. Ensure that teachers carry out the supervisory duties and instructional program assigned by the principal and supply such information as the principal may require.

5. Staff Supervision

a. Supervise the instruction in the school.

b. Assign duties to the vice-principal. A vice-principal shall perform such duties as are assigned by the principal. In the absence of the principal of a school, a vice-principal, where a vice-principal has been appointed for the school, shall be in charge of the school and shall perform the duties of the principal.

c. Administratively supervise psychiatrists, psychologists, social workers, and other professional support staff where such persons are performing their duties in the school.

d. Assign duties to vice-principals and teachers in charge.

6. Staff Evaluation

a. Conduct performance appraisals of "new teachers" as mandated by district contract.

b. Conduct performance appraisals of all teachers as mandated by district contract.

c. If a performance appraisal is unsatisfactory, the principal must
   (i) document concerns;
   (ii) consult regularly with his or her supervisor regarding the teacher's performance and steps that may be taken to improve it; and
   (iii) provide feedback and recommendations to the teacher to help improve the teacher's performance.

7. Staff Cooperation

a. Ensure that principals and teachers display personal and professional qualities.

b. Establish and maintain mutually respectful relationships with students, staff, and parents.

8. **School Administration**

   a. Maintain student records including attendance.

   b. Examine all data in a timely manner.

   c. Enforce all local policy and codes of conduct.

9. **Access to School**

   a. Monitor visitors into the school (i.e., visitor's book).

   b. Monitor student health records according to district policy.

   c. Direct a person to leave the school premises if the principal believes that the person is prohibited by regulation or under a district policy from being there.

10. **Building Maintenance**

    a. Monitor condition and maintenance of property.

    b. Inspect the school premises regularly and make reports to appropriate officials.

    c. Provide appropriate facilities for instruction and other activities.

11. **Community**

    a. Promote and maintain close cooperation with community and business.

    b. Promote and maintain close cooperation with the parents and guardians.

12. **School Advisory Group**

    a. Act as resource person to any school advisory groups, and assist such groups in obtaining information.

    b. Solicit views with respect to local code of conduct, school policies respecting appropriate dress, and school action plans for improvement based on data.

    c. Consider recommendations and advice when determining action to be taken in response.

13. Reports to District

a. Report to supervisors as required.

b. Transmit reports and recommendations to the district through the appropriate supervisor.

Always Put the Students First

Always put the students first in any decision that you make. Let this be the philosophy upon which you structure the school.

Establish a strong vision that puts student well-being and achievement first, and use that as your guide when dealing with parents and staff.

The Voice of Experience

Legal Framework

HIERARCHICAL LEGISLATIVE FRAMEWORK: AN OVERVIEW

> The key is to follow your district school board's policies and procedures; they are consistent with *all* relevant legislation.

TIPS

All of your day-to-day duties, responsibilities, and activities are carried out within a hierarchical legislative framework.

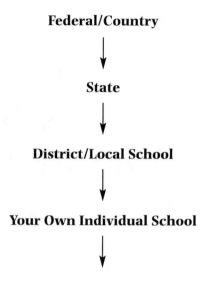

Federal/Country

Example: Charter of Rights and Freedoms

State

Examples:

1. Education acts and regulations

2. Human rights codes

3. Other relevant acts and regulations

District School Boards

District school boards develop and approve policies and procedures with respect to duties and responsibilities placed upon them by legislation.

- **Policies** provide general direction and set broad guidelines for behavior within the district.

- **Procedures** spell out how the policies will be enacted within various district settings.

In general, policies dictate what to do, and procedures describe in detail how to do it.

School district policies are often grouped together into sections or areas, for example, School Operations. Each policy is linked to a procedure. One policy in the School Operations section might be a Student Dress Code to establish expectations for appropriate dress within all the schools of the district and to provide directions for the development, implementation, and review of individual school dress codes. A corresponding district procedure would then be created to provide a detailed description of the process to be followed in developing, implementing, and reviewing a student dress code within each individual school.

Individual Schools: Policies, Procedures, and Rules

School Policies and Procedures

Individual schools create and implement their own policies and procedures, which must be consistent with district school policies, for example, a schoolwide homework policy, or a set of procedures for students to sign in late.

School Rules

Individual schools also establish their own rules with specific expectations for behavior, accompanied by clear consequences. Rules may be specific to particular schools, but must not contradict district policy. For example, pupils at one school may be allowed to wear hats in class, while at another school in the same district they may not.

Always Put the Students First

Never take the easiest solution to a difficult problem; it is seldom the best solution. Always do the hard thing, the right thing, the ethical thing.

Make sure all school decisions are made in the best interests of your students.

— *The Voice of Experience*

Negligence and Liability

3

At a Glance

- First Steps to Reduce Risk
    Review District Policies and Procedures
    Review, Communicate, and
        Monitor School Policies and Procedures
    Develop the Documentation Habit
    Encourage Staff to Keep Up-to-Date
- Negligence: An Overview of the Concepts and Issues
    Negligence
    Duty of Care
    Standard of Care
- Duty to Provide Adequate Supervision of Pupils

➔ FIRST STEPS TO REDUCE RISK

You, the staff, the students, and their parents all desire and deserve a safe teaching and learning environment in the school.

The steps you take to promote a safe environment will reduce the risk of injury or loss.

Here are some initial steps you can take to reduce the risk of injury and loss, and thus reduce the risk of legal liability.

Review District Policies and Procedures

- It is critical to know and follow your district policies and procedures, especially those related to higher risk activities, for example, field trips and administering medication to students.

- Report to senior administration in writing any concerns you have regarding your ability to implement the district policies and procedures.

Review, Communicate, and Monitor School Policies and Procedures

- Review

  1. Do the school policies, procedures, and practices follow district policies and procedures?

  2. Does the school handbook reflect district policies?

- Communicate

  1. Inform staff, students, and parents at the start of the school year and on an ongoing basis.

  2. Discuss issues regularly with school staff, parents, and volunteers.

  3. Document staff discussions (e.g., items on staff meeting agenda, references in staff meeting minutes).

  4. File memos to staff, parents, and volunteers.

- Monitor

  1. Monitor and ensure compliance.

  2. Document in your Day-Timer or organizer conversations you have with individual staff members regarding concerns and actions taken.

  3. Be mindful of collective agreements and union relations.

Develop the Documentation Habit

- Written records must be specific; note the date, time, place, and people involved.

- Be accurate and factual, and record what was said.

- Be objective. Do not include personal opinions and value judgments.

Members of the teaching profession must be increasingly diligent about documenting all controversial phone calls, meetings, and events.

Encourage Staff to Keep Up-to-Date

Encourage teachers to keep up-to-date on curriculum and safety issues by joining professional associations.

NEGLIGENCE: AN OVERVIEW OF THE CONCEPTS AND ISSUES

Negligence

Negligence is concerned with unintentional acts or omissions that may cause a loss or injury. In general, you will not be found liable for negligence unless it is proven that

- there was a duty of care toward the plaintiff (e.g., the student);
- there was a breach of the duty of care owed;
- the breach was the proximate cause of the loss or injury; and
- there was actual damage or loss as a result of the injury.

Negligence is the omission to do something which a reasonable man, guided upon those considerations which ordinarily regulate the conduct of human affairs, would do, or doing something which a prudent and reasonable man would not do.

—*Blyth v. Birmingham Water Works Co.*,
as quoted in *Legal Handbook for Educators*,
A. F. Brown, p. 102

Duty of Care

Principals, teachers, and school districts owe a duty of care to their students; that is, a duty to ensure the students' safety and well-being. In addition, you and your staff act *in loco parentis* (in the place of a parent); therefore you owe a common law duty of care to students as well.

Standard of Care

The standard of care you owe your students is that of a reasonably careful or prudent guardian in similar circumstances. The standard of care owed to students varies in different circumstances (e.g., in the gym, science lab, or regular classroom; in the school yard; on a field trip). Consider the factors listed by Mr. Justice McIntyre (1981) as quoted below by Roher and Wormwell in *An Educator's Guide to the Role of the Principal*, pp. 45–46:

- The number of students being supervised at any given time

- The nature of the exercise or activity in progress

- The age of the student

- The degree of skill and training that the students may have received in connection with the activity

- The nature and condition of the equipment in use at the time

- The competence and capacity of the students involved

> You have a duty to provide appropriate and reasonable supervision of pupils at the school. If you believe that particular circumstances exist at your school that prevent you from carrying out that duty, contact your superintendent of schools.

DUTY TO PROVIDE ADEQUATE SUPERVISION OF PUPILS

1. **Ensure** that

    a. A supervision program and a duty schedule are in place

    b. Both regular and occasional staff know their duties

    c. The supervision program complies with collective agreements and district policies and procedures

2. **Consider** specific supervision requirements, for example,

    a. Critical times
       (i) In the schoolyard or building before and immediately after school
       (ii) At recess and lunch hour

   b. Critical areas

     (i) In hallways and lunchrooms or cafeteria

     (ii) At bus arrival and departure zones

   c. Special situations

     (i) School assemblies and dances, inclement weather, early dismissals

     (ii) Circumstances particular to your students, school, or community

3. Follow the elements of a reasonable supervision policy:

   a. Applicable district policies and procedures

   b. Supervision routines for particular activities or areas

   c. Instructions to staff and students about expected conduct

   d. Consideration of the ratio of supervisors to students for particular activities

   e. Consideration of any inherent dangers

   f. Any special circumstances of individual students

   g. Weather conditions for outdoor activities

   h. The geography of the area to be supervised

SOURCE (Item C): Adapted from J. C. Batzel, Negligence and the Liability of School Boards and Teachers Towards Students, as quoted in *An Educator's Guide to the Role of the Principal,* E. M. Roher and S. A. Wormwell, p. 54.

4. Conduct a site safety audit:

   a. Take into consideration such factors as lines of sight when developing the supervision plan.

   b. Use your district school board's safety guidelines.

What will constitute adequate supervision of pupils?

Advice

Although principals have overall responsibility for the supervision of pupils, most direct supervision is provided by other district employees and volunteers. The principal's duty to supervise pupils is therefore often subsumed in the duty to supervise these other people. (Note: The principal's duty to supervise pupils also requires that adequate supervision, in terms of numbers, is in place.)

In addition to students, principals also have the following people under their professional supervision: teachers, vice-principals, educational assistants and other on-site learning or behavior resource staff, secretarial and custodial staff, school guests, and volunteers.

Complying with relevant acts and regulations, following district school board policies and procedures, and exercising good judgment and common sense will all help to significantly reduce the risk of legal liability.

Seminars, conferences, and reading current publications are the keys to effective decisions.

Make Decisions Wisely

Take the time needed to make thoughtful decisions. Never make hasty decisions.

Give yourself time to reflect and perhaps even sleep on it.

Don't make a difficult decision today that can wait until tomorrow.
 Be sure to gather all the facts.
 Try to have a cool-off period if you're under duress.
 Phone a colleague—just to be sure.
 Base your decision on common sense and how it will help kids.

The Voice of Experience

Management  Skills

 ## MANAGERIAL EXCELLENCE AND
SCHOOL LEADERSHIP: AN OVERVIEW

Managerial excellence is one of six areas of school leadership.

The challenge is to develop skills for managing the improvement of student learning.

—*A New Time—A New Schoolhouse Leader,*
A. J. H. Newberry, p. 45

23

As a principal, you exercise your leadership and management skills every day.

Leadership

1. Leadership relates to mission, direction and inspiration.

—*An Educator's Guide to the Role of the Principal*,
E. M. Roher and S. A. Wormwell, p. 2

2. Leaders do the right thing.

Management

1. Management involves designing and carrying out plans, getting things done and working effectively with people.

2. Managers do things right.

—*Leaders: The Strategies for Taking Charge*,
W. Bennis and B. Nanus, p. 21

The following are three skill sets that can enhance your effectiveness:

1. Time management

2. Delegation

3. Visibility

TIME MANAGEMENT

Time management techniques strive to

- reduce redundant efforts;
- eliminate unnecessary routine and paper work;
- set operational priorities;
- focus attention.

SOURCE: Adapted from *Principals for Our Changing Schools: The Knowledge and Skill Base*, S. D. Thompson, p. 5-15.

➔ Getting Started

The biggest time management challenge is ensuring that you take control of your own time; it is possible to do this. Your other major challenge is identifying and focusing on what's important, rather than on busywork.

Your Desk: A Good Place to Start

TIPS

Your desk may be the best place to start your commitment to improved time management skills.

Your desk needs to be set up to meet your needs.

Committing to a clean desk policy and a well-organized workspace will help get you off to a good start.

Setting Up Your Office

1. **Maximize efficiency:**

   Keep the files and materials that you use most frequently at your desk.

   Program the speed-dial numbers on your phone.

   Organize your workspace for efficient accessibility.

2. **Maximize personal safety and security:**

   Consider lines of sight, exits, and other safety issues when configuring your office.

   Plan for both open-door and closed-door meetings.

   Install a window in solid doors.

   Set up procedures for office staff to monitor your meetings with difficult people.

3. **Plan your office to convey the image and message you wish to project.**

➔ Nine Principles of Time Management: An Overview

1. Establish priorities.

2. Welcome routines and procedures.

3. Transfer your "monkeys" to someone else's back.

4. Delegate, delegate, delegate. (See the Delegation section of this chapter.)

5. Manage incoming mail and phone calls.

6. Organize your paper work and your workspace.

7. Use time in large chunks when necessary.

8. Learn to say no.

9. Estimate your time needs.

SOURCE: Adapted from *The New Manager's Starter Kit*, R. Crittendon, pp. 34–35.

> Your success comes down to the difference between managing your work and letting your work manage you.

Doing the Right Job at the Right Time: More Time Management Tips

1. Plan daily routine around important tasks.

2. Review to-do list throughout the day.

tomorrow's agenda before you leave.

3. Monitor time spent on low priority items (e.g., reading the mail, answering e-mail, talking on the phone).

time spent on the most important tasks.

4. Don't just react to events as they occur. Take a proactive approach to your day.

use routine interruptions (e.g., the arrival of the mail) as an excuse to avoid important tasks.

ignore little problems; they may become big ones.

5. Do allow time for unexpected problems and essential interruptions.

allow more time than you think you'll need for each task.

set aside time by yourself to work on major projects whenever necessary.

Do it, or delegate it. File it, or throw it out.

For further information on time management and routines, see Appendix B: "Principals' Routines" and Appendix C: "Regular Monthly Activities for Principals."

DELEGATION

Delegation is an essential strategy that many new administrators have difficulty putting into practice; yet it is an effective way to save time and enhance leadership capacity within the school.

> —Three Days of Learning: Quick Tips and
> Techniques Provided to the Principal in
> Action, L. Hodgins, *The Register,* October 2001, p. 24

Delegation is important. You cannot do all the work yourself. Take care not to delegate too many tasks to just one or two willing and able people. Try to involve as many staff members as appropriate.

Seven Dimensions of Delegation and Related Key Behaviors of Effective Principals

1. **Task Identification**

   - Show confidence in yourself and be willing to let others assume authority.

   - Identify tasks appropriate for staff and beneficial to the school.

   - Assume responsibility for tasks functionally limited to the principal (e.g., teacher evaluation).

   - Maintain the symbolic leadership role (e.g., presenting important awards to students and staff).

2. **Identification of Delegatees**

   - Identify delegatees appropriate for the task or tasks.

   - Consider the stage of career development of the delegatee.

- View delegation assignments as staff development opportunities as well as task accomplishment.
- Delegate tasks to the level nearest the action or concern (e.g., to teachers, vice-principal, or support staff).

3. **Authority and Responsibility**

- Delegate authority sufficient to accomplish the mission.
- Accept different approaches or different conclusions.
- Specify the limits of delegatee authority.
- Clarify delegatee accountability to the principal.

4. **Support and Feedback**

- Make available necessary resources (e.g., information, time, money, equipment, support services, facilities).
- Provide training.
- Maintain active interest and seek feedback.
- Make the school and community aware of the delegatees and their mission(s).

5. **Participation and Autonomy**

- Facilitate task accomplishment without interfering in the delegatees' work.
- Involve other individuals or groups in decisions as the work evolves.
- Maintain active communication with delegatees.

6. **Accountability**

- Plan the review and reporting process for the delegated task or project.
- Focus on results rather than process.
- Exhibit confidence in delegatees.
- Tailor the level of accountability to the experience of the delegatee and the significance of the task.

7. **Assessment**

- Assess participant performance.
- Act on task results.
- Recognize accomplishments of individuals and groups.
- Organize closure activity as appropriate.

SOURCE: Adapted from *Principals for Our Changing Schools: The Knowledge and Skill Base*, S. D. Thompson, pp. 7-10 to 7-15.

> ## Decide what you are not going to do.
>
> The principal's job is to ensure that essential things get done, not to do them all himself or herself.
>
> —*What's Worth Fighting For in the Principalship?*
> M. Fullan, p. 36

TIPS Four Delegation Tips

1. Myths about delegation:

You can't trust your employees to be responsible.

When you delegate you lose control of a task and its outcome.

You are the only one who has all the answers.

You can do all the work faster by yourself.

Delegation dilutes your authority.

Your employees will be recognized for doing a good job, but you won't.

Delegation decreases your flexibility.

Your employees are too busy.

Your workers don't see the big picture.

2. The six steps of delegating:

Communicate the task.

Furnish context for the task.

Determine standards.

Grant authority.

Provide support.

Get commitment.

3. Delegate these things:

Detail work

Information gathering

Repetitive assignments

Surrogate roles (employees fill in for you at a meeting if appropriate)

Future duties (to give employees a taste of their own future duties)

4. **Do not delegate these things:**

> Long-term vision and goals
>
> Performance appraisals, discipline, and counseling
>
> Politically sensitive situations
>
> Personal assignments
>
> Issues with confidential or sensitive circumstances

SOURCE: Adapted from *Managing for Dummies*, B. Nelson and P. Economy, pp. 48–59.

> Be visible; do not delegate important symbolic tasks. You can, however, share these tasks.

VISIBILITY: MANAGEMENT BY WALKING AROUND

TIPS

> While you are engaged in "management by walking around," you have a perfect opportunity to walk your talk, to demonstrate through your words and actions the attitudes and behaviors that the school values. As the principal, you are a significant role model, and you will have a positive impact on the behavior of others by visibly modeling desired behaviors yourself.

An Overview

1. Practice planned visibility systematically so that students, teachers, and the community know you care and are present.

2. Be visible in classrooms, in hallways, on the playground, in the cafeteria, at staff workshops, etc.

3. Your symbolic presence at school events sends a message of concern and interest.

4. Visibility throughout the school day helps reduce student discipline problems, sets school tone, and promotes communication.

5. High visibility is a natural expression of concern and interest.

Visibility—getting out of the office and being seen all over the school—was the most frequently identified quality of a strong school leader.

—Education World survey of principals, as reported by the National Association of Elementary School Principals on its Web site (www.NAESP.org)

TIPS Planned Visibility: Ten Practical Tips

Being visible promotes good communication. Positive, proactive communication can be a very enjoyable part of your school day, and it pays enormous dividends.

1. Get to know the names of all staff members and students as soon as possible.

2. Walk the halls before school in the morning; stop into classrooms to chat with staff.

3. Allow time for casual, informal encounters with staff members throughout the day.

4. Schedule times every day when you are in the hallways, schoolyard, cafeteria, etc.

5. Meet the school buses as they arrive, and greet the students.

6. Chat with parents as they drop students off in the morning or pick them up at night.

7. Visit the gym, library, and school foyer whenever possible during the day; talk with students.

8. Go outside frequently during recesses and the lunch hour.

9. Put yourself on the duty schedule; bus duty or early morning hall duty can work well.

10. Be highly visible. The more you are out and about, the more opportunities there are for positive, face-to-face communication. (If you're out of sight, you'll be out of touch.)

A final word: Be sure when you are out and about in the school that you spend time in classrooms informally observing students and teachers at work.

Delegate

If you haven't learned how to prioritize and delegate, do so quickly.

Offer those following you the leadership opportunities you were given. You cannot do it all yourself. Teamwork is the key.

Don't overload your willing horses.

The Voice of Experience

Communication

At a Glance

- Communication Tips and Checklists
  Be Visible
  Practice Active Listening
  Communication: Ten Basic Tips
  Hierarchy of Effective Communication
  Who Are Your Target Audiences?
  Methods of Communication
- Written Communication
  Documents Inventory: 20 Forms of Written Communication
  Speaking Versus Writing
  Reasons for Putting It in Writing
  Tips for Communicating by E-Mail
- School Newsletters
  Tips for Writing School Newsletters
  The Effectiveness of School Newsletters
  Distribution of School Newsletters
- School Communication Plan

COMMUNICATION TIPS AND CHECKLISTS

Be Visible

Positive, proactive communication can be a very enjoyable part of your school day, and it pays enormous dividends. Being visible promotes good communication. See "Planned Visibility: Ten Practical Tips" in Chapter 4.

Practice Active Listening

One of the best ways you can establish yourself in your new school is to practice active listening. When you are building relationships, how well you listen is as important as what you say and how you say it. When you practice active listening, you make statements that encourage others to talk.

TIPS *Active Listening Techniques: Six Tips*

1. Encourage

- Draw the other person out.

- Use verbal and nonverbal cues to show that you are really listening.

- Convey attentiveness with body language and short vocal responses.

- Be aware that appropriate body language and vocalizations vary from culture to culture.

    Examples: "Can you tell me more?"
    "I'd like to hear about this."

2. Clarify

- Ask questions to confirm what the speaker has said.

- Not only will this help you to understand, but it may also help the speaker examine his or her own perceptions.

    Examples: "Could you tell me which of those things happened first?"
    "When did this happen?"

3. Restate

- Repeat in your words what the speaker has said.

- This shows you are listening and helps check for facts and meaning.

    Examples: "She told you she'd call right back and called two days later."
    "So you'd like your parent to trust you more, is that right?"

4. Reflect

- In your own words, tell what you think the speaker is experiencing.

- This can lead the speaker to be more expressive.

- It also provides a way to check the accuracy of your perceptions.

    Examples: "You seem quite upset."
    "It sounds like you felt really humiliated."

5. Summarize

- Reiterate the major ideas, themes, and feelings that the speaker has expressed.

- This provides review and a basis from which to continue the dialogue.

  Examples: "So the main problems you have with this are . . . ."
  "These seem to be the key ideas you've expressed."

6. Validate

- Show appreciation for the speaker's efforts.

- Acknowledge the value of talking.

- Affirm your positive feelings about being part of the dialogue.

  Examples: "I'm really glad we're talking."
  "I appreciate your willingness to resolve this."

> Don't just hear—listen.
> Listen constantly. Listen carefully. Listen thoughtfully.
> Listen and learn.

Communication: Ten Basic Tips

1. Make communications a focus.

2. Do not substitute technology for communication. Technology is an effective tool, not a substitute for good interpersonal communication.

3. Consider who needs to know what, and how and when they will receive the information.

4. Keep your communication as positive as possible. Avoid knee-jerk negative responses.

5. If you are asked a question and you don't have the answer, respond with "I don't know, but I'll find out."

6. Be sensitive to misinterpretation of your writing. For example, written correspondence and e-mail that you may have written casually may be taken very seriously by the recipient. Give each message a second reading. Read it from the recipient's perspective.

7. Don't fabricate excuses to cover your mistakes.

8. It's alright to change your mind when new evidence comes to light, as long as you don't do it so often that you are labeled indecisive.

9. Don't take yourself too seriously. (Take your work seriously, but not yourself.)

10. Once again, never underestimate the importance of communication.

SOURCE: Adapted from *The New Manager's Starter Kit*, R. Crittendon, pp. 9–13.

Hierarchy of Effective Communication

Below are 10 methods of communication, listed from most to least effective:

1. One-to-one or face-to-face communication

2. Small group discussions and meetings

3. Speaking before a large group

4. Telephone conversations

5. Handwritten personal notes

6. Typewritten, personal letters (not computer generated form letters)

7. Computer generated "personalized" letters

8. Brochures or pamphlets distributed by mail

9. Articles in organizational newsletters, magazines, or tabloids

10. News releases carried in local newspapers, including various ethno-cultural papers

School Web Site

Your school Web site is a highly visible and very public form of communication.

- Keep protection of privacy in mind as you post items to the site.

- Check your district protocols.

- Be sure to assign responsibility for regular monitoring and updating of the school site.

✓ Who Are Your Target Audiences?

Always ask yourself: With *whom* should I communicate in this particular situation?

Consider students, staff, others at the school, parents, the school advisory group, your district school board, other agencies, your professional associations, the community, and the media.

1. Students

Students

Students' advisory group

2. School-Based Staff

Administrative assistants

Audiovisual technicians

Computer technicians

Custodians (day and evening)

Educational assistants

Library technicians

Occasional teachers

Occupational health and safety representative

Teachers

Union stewards

Vice-principals

3. Others at School

Bus drivers

Co-op students

Crossing guards

Evening rental groups

Evening security guards

Food service personnel

Multicultural liaison officers

Staff of on-site child care (preschool, before- and after-school programs)

Student teachers

4. **Parents and Guardians**

Foster parents

Parent volunteers in the school

Parents of all students

5. **School Advisory Group**

All school advisory group members

Community representative

School advisory group chair

Staff representatives on school advisory group

Student representative

6. **District School Board**

District superintendent of schools

District psychologist or social worker assigned to your school

District staff (e.g., transportation)

District school board trustees

Other principals in the district

Other schools in the neighborhood

7. **Other Agencies**

Children's Aid Society/Child and Family Services agencies

Local fire department

Local police department

Other community and social services

Probation services

Public health unit

Senior administration

8. Professional Associations

National Association of Secondary School Principals

National Association of Elementary School Principals

Ontario Principals' Council

Canadian Association of Principals

National Association of Head Teachers

Local principals' organization

Other professional associations

9. Community

Community members with children no longer in the school system

Community members without children

Households adjacent to the schoolyard

Local businesses

Local community groups (ethnic, cultural, religious, recreational)

Local government

Professional associations

Service clubs, Rotary, Kiwanis

10. Media

Local newspaper

Local radio

Local television

Methods of Communication

Always ask yourself: *How* should I communicate in this particular situation?

1. Written Communication

Memos

Letters

E-mail

Daily or weekly bulletins for staff

Wall-size master calendar and individual copies

Notices posted on bulletin boards or white board in staff room or elsewhere

Information placed in individual staff mailboxes

Notices posted on school intranet for staff

Outdoor portable sign on lawn or roof for specific events (can be rented)

2. Informal Oral Communication

Passing conversations in hallway, schoolyard, or parking lot

Brief one-on-one chats in office or classroom

3. Meetings

Scheduled one-on-one meetings

Staff meetings

Team meetings

Committee meetings

Large assemblies and student/parent evenings

4. Formal Oral Communication

Individual phone calls

Recorded messages on school phone

Telephone tree

Computer programmed automated telephone dial-out messaging system

Morning announcements over the P.A. system

TIPS
Keep your supervisory officer informed about emerging issues. No one likes unpleasant surprises. Give your supervisor a heads-up if something is simmering or has just boiled over.

WRITTEN COMMUNICATION

Documents Inventory:
Twenty Forms of Written Communication

As a principal, your written communication takes many different forms, including those below:

1. **Agendas and minutes**: staff meetings, committee meetings

2. **Articles** for professional journals

3. **Funding proposals** and requests for school pilot projects

4. **General letters**: welcome to parents new to the school

5. **Newsletter**: staff newsletter, school newsletter

6. **Handbooks**: teacher, student, parent

7. **Information brochures** and packages regarding school programs

8. **Letters of acknowledgment**

9. **Letters of recommendation**: staff, students, others

10. **Memos**: written reinforcement of verbal requests, general directions

11. **News releases** for local media (For further details see Chapter 6: "Public and Media Relations.")

12. **Proposals for presentations** in local or national conferences

13. **Reports**: staff performance appraisal reports

14. **School plans**: professional development, school improvement, communication

15. **Special occasion cards**, get-well cards, birthday cards

16. **Summaries**: written summaries of district school board meetings, school advisory group meetings

17. **Surveys**: staff, student, parent, and community surveys (Consult the research and evaluation department in your district for assistance in developing survey instruments.)

18. **Thank you notes** (handwritten) to staff, students, volunteers, others

19. **Translations**: key parent communications translated into other languages

20. **Written responses** (if appropriate) to parent concerns and questions

> This list can serve as a memory jogger when you are selecting artifacts for your professional portfolio.

Speaking Versus Writing

When should you give a message orally and when should you put it in writing?

1. Your choice will depend on
   - how much time you have,
   - how important the message is,
   - the attitude and nature of your intended receiver(s),
   - whether you want to keep a permanent record.

2. You may want to send a message orally when
   - you want immediate and direct feedback,
   - you don't want a written record (if writing will commit you too firmly to a course of action and take away your options or flexibility),
   - there is not enough time to put something in writing,
   - delivering the message in person will increase its impact or urgency.

3. You may want to write a message when
   - several people must act on the same instructions;
   - there are regulatory, legal, or contractual requirements involved;
   - you want to take a formal position on the matter, clarify an opinion, or dispel a rumor;
   - you want to provide a precise set of instructions;
   - the receiver tends to disregard or forget oral instructions.

SOURCE: Adapted from *The Rookie Manager,* J. Straub, pp. 150–151.

Document, Document, Document **TIPS**

Document all meetings, conversations, telephone calls, and incidents that have any possibility of future concern, contention, or controversy.

✓ Reasons for Putting It in Writing

1. To refresh your memory

2. To allow time to reread, absorb, and consider facts and ideas

3. To document occurrences, behaviors, meetings

4. To assure accuracy of records; to keep lists of facts, dates, figures

5. To give or receive orders or instructions

6. To prepare reports (e.g., accident reports)

7. To prevent misunderstandings

8. To save time; to plan ahead; to organize

9. To state or to confirm an agreement

10. To keep track of what has been said

Source: *Think Like a Manager,* R. Fritz, p. 240.

Unless there is a specific reason to put a communication in writing, don't. **TIPS**

1. Give priority to face-to-face communication.

2. Communication by phone should generally be your second choice.

3. If your district has a form for documenting particular circumstances, use it.

4. Do document all your significant meetings, whether in person or by phone.

5. When you send a written communication to someone, consider whether e-mail or hard copy is more appropriate.

6. When you do put something in writing, edit, rewrite, and reread it again (at a later time if possible) before sending it.

7. Time is almost always on your side, so don't rush important written communications.

8. Many things that you write can be used for several purposes, with little or no modification. This can be a great time saver. For example, a brief overview of the new math curriculum can be used in the school newsletter, as an introduction to the course outline, and as a handout at a curriculum evening or school advisory group presentation.

9. Save electronic copies (and hard copies where appropriate) of letters, reports, newsletters, etc., and use them as templates in the future.

10. Use the sample letters created by your district (e.g., for suspensions).

Tips Tips for Communicating by E-Mail

Tone

- Avoid jokes or sarcasm; what you find funny may be obnoxious or offensive to others.

- Be careful about your message's tone; it is easy for someone to misinterpret it.

- If your message is very important, controversial, or confidential or could be easily misunderstood, use the telephone or set up a face-to-face meeting.

- Send positive messages so recipients will look forward to receiving them.

- To communicate a negative message, pick up the phone, or even better, schedule a face-to-face meeting.

- When writing e-mail messages, use the same diction and common sense you would use if you were writing a letter, talking on the phone, or meeting face-to-face.

Format

- Create a signature file to automatically appear at the bottom of each of your messages: your name, title, school, address and e-mail address, and phone.

- Keep the message short and simple.

- Put the most important information in the first line of the first paragraph.

- When you send or receive an e-mail message that contains important information, save a copy on your hard drive and/or print out a copy and file it.

- Write a subject line that is descriptive (e.g., "attend Tues. meeting at 9:30").

- Write messages that are easy to respond to; readers can reply *yes* or *no*.

Audience

- If it's not necessary to respond to each and every e-mail message, don't.

- Don't send copies to people who don't need to see your message.

Etiquette

- Always reread your e-mail message before sending it.

- Beware of crying wolf; use the *Urgent Message* notation sparingly.

- Don't write e-mail messages using all capital letters; it's known as shouting.

- Remember: e-mail messages are not private. Never write anything in an e-mail message that you would not want to become public.

- Run your spell-checker and proofread your message.

- The fewer messages you send, the greater the attention they will receive.

Note: You may not want to start active e-mail correspondence with hundreds of parents; it can be overwhelming. However, e-mail is a great way to communicate with staff members.

Know the difference between *Reply Sender* and *Reply All*. Be careful every time.

SCHOOL NEWSLETTERS

 Tips for Writing School Newsletters

1. Check your district procedures with respect to use of students' names and photos.

2. Adopt a catchy name and logo and a readily identified masthead.

3. Use bold attention-getting headlines.

4. Adopt a right-to-the-point writing style.

5. Share your personal priorities as the school leader.

6. Insert clip-and-save calendars.

7. When reproducing materials, don't break copyright laws.

8. Include lots of student quotes, student writing, and examples of student work.

9. Include photos and reproductions of student artwork.

10. Leave plenty of white space.

11. Include items that reinforce school curriculum and learning.

12. Publish regularly.

13. Consider publishing your newsletter by e-mail or on school home page if your community is online.

14. Use tear sheets to generate feedback and two-way communication; seek feedback. (To encourage response, put returns into a draw for a prize.)

15. Proofread, proofread, proofread.

16. Try to avoid jargon and acronyms, running too long (consider a one-pager with calendar on reverse), talking down to readers.

Note: Be sure to have appropriate prior permission before including students' names, photos, work samples, etc., in your newsletter.

If you publish your newsletter electronically or post it to your school Web site, extra care is required regarding the inclusion of photos of students or students' names.

The Effectiveness of School Newsletters

Parents learn about their children's schools through many sources:

1. Conversations with their children

2. Their children's report cards

3. The school newsletter

4. Parent-teacher conferences

5. Personal visits to the school

6. Teacher notes and phone calls

7. Conversations with friends and neighbors

8. Meet-the-teacher night

9. Open houses at the school

10. Local newspapers

✓ Distribution of School Newsletters

Arrange with several principals to send school newsletters to each other every month.

Develop a distribution list for your school newsletter that includes:

1. Parents

2. Staff

3. District staff who visit your school regularly (e.g., a social worker)

4. Bus drivers

5. Superintendent of schools

6. Community representative on school advisory group

7. Community businesses or associations

8. Other schools in your area

9. Day care or other programs operating in the school

10. Trustee(s) (if appropriate in your district)

SCHOOL COMMUNICATION PLAN

Develop a school communication plan.

1. In every situation you face, consider these five key questions:

    a. *What* information do you want to communicate?

    b. *Why* do you want to communicate the information?

    c. *Who* needs to receive the information?

    d. *How* should the information be communicated?

    e. *When* should the information be communicated?

2. When developing your school communication plan, ask the following six questions:

    a. Who is my audience?

    b. What is my key message?

    c. What strategy/vehicle will be successful?

    d. Who is responsible?

    e. What are the timelines?

    f. How will I measure success?

Your communication plan might follow a format similar to the one below.

Audience	Key Messages	Strategies	Person Responsible	Timelines
–				
–				
–				
–				
–				

For more information on developing a school communication plan, see "Building a Public Relations Program for Your School" in Chapter 6.

Also, see Chapter 9, "Records and Information Management," for further information regarding confidentiality and communication, and Chapter 25, "Emergency Preparedness," for further information regarding crisis communication.

Communicate Constantly

Remember: As the school leader, there are certain things that are not appropriate for you to say.

Build strong relationships with parents and the community; the rewards for the students and the school are endless.

Appreciate the value of listening. Colleagues, parents, and students all need to feel they have been heard before they feel ready to listen. Practice active listening.

The Voice of Experience

Public and Media Relations

6

At a Glance

- Building a Public Relations Program for Your School
- Tips for Writing a News Release
- Tips for Giving Media Interviews
  Before the Interview
  During the Interview
  Media Interview Do's and Don'ts

BUILDING A PUBLIC RELATIONS PROGRAM FOR YOUR SCHOOL

Public Relations

Principals need to be able to change negative attitudes and build on positive ones to develop public support for education in general and schools in particular.

This support must be earned on an ongoing basis throughout the school year.

Public relations is the vehicle through which this occurs.

> A good public relations plan centers on communicating, educating and influencing your school community.
>
> *—Principals for Our Changing Schools:*
> *The Knowledge and Skill Base,*
> S. D. Thompson, pp. 21–23

1. When developing your school's public relations program, keep in mind that such plans

   - Require a community focus

   - Are low-cost and practical

   - Require that parents play a key role in relationships with the school

   - Recognize staff communication as the starting point for all public relations activities

   - Manage crises to limit damage to the school's reputation

   - Require that principals work effectively with the media

   - Utilize technology to improve their effectiveness

SOURCE: *Principals for Our Changing Schools: The Knowledge and Skill Base*, S. D. Thompson, pp. 21–25.

Remember

1. Effective public relations programs begin with effective staff communication.

2. Always communicate internally (with your entire staff) before communicating externally.

2. Before building your school's public relations plan, you need to be aware of your district's communication and public relations protocols. Check your district's policies and procedures regarding public relations and communications. Find out who the communications officers are in your district. Determine their responsibilities:

   - Do they write news releases?

   - Are they the media spokespersons for your school?

- Can you talk to the media yourself?

- How do they promote individual school stories?

- Do they need to see and sign off on materials such as news releases before the materials are released to the media?

Arrange to meet with your district's communications officer to establish a personal connection.

3. Be sure your school communication plan identifies ways to

- Provide complete, accurate information to staff in a timely manner

- Obtain feedback from staff and establish effective two-way communication

- Seek the advice and input of staff right from the start, as you design your school's public relations program

4. When building your school's public relations plan, seek feedback from the parents as well. You might use

- A suggestion box in the school office or library

- A return tear sheet in the newsletter

- A dedicated voice mailbox

- Your school Web site

- Brief questionnaires or surveys (Contact your district's research and evaluation department for assistance in developing the questionnaires.)

5. Communication plans and public relations programs must provide many opportunities

- To listen

- To receive as well as send information

- To promote two-way communication

TIPS TIPS FOR WRITING A NEWS RELEASE

Make sure your story is newsworthy. (Ask yourself: Would I be interested in this if I were not a principal?)

Keep it short and punchy to grab attention. Limit your news release to one page, if possible. Consider adding a fact sheet as supplementary information.

Summarize the most important facts about the story—the who, what, where, when, and why—in your lead paragraph.

Use a catchy headline to summarize your story and capture the recipient's attention.

Include a quote. Reporters will often take a quote directly from the release, so providing one helps get your message out in your own words.

Ensure the information is timely. All media outlets are bound by deadlines. Find out what the deadlines are, and be strategic in releasing your information.

Always put a date on your release.

Check the accuracy of your information. Double-check your facts and figures, and attribute third party information to a legitimate source.

Make sure the information is easy to read and to understand—avoid education jargon and acronyms.

Include a contact person and phone number in case journalists need additional information.

Target your efforts. Take time to find out who covers education and direct your material to that specific individual. (Keep your media lists current; media people tend to move around a lot.)

Watch your spelling and grammar; check for typos.

Ⓣⓘⓟⓢ TIPS FOR GIVING MEDIA INTERVIEWS

Before the Interview

When approached by the media to give an interview, collect the following information:

1. What is the name, phone number, and fax number of the reporter?

2. What is the name of the media outlet?

3. What is the subject of the interview?

4. What is the specific angle?

5. What is the reporter's real deadline?

6. How long will the interview last and where will it be conducted? (This will need to be negotiated.)

7. Who else will the reporter be talking to?

8. Can you provide them with some background information in advance?

9. What kind of story is this—feature, business, social, political?

10. Is there anything else you can tell me about this?

Give yourself time to prepare for the interview:

1. Talk to others in the school if they are involved in the issue.

2. Prepare for the toughest questions.

3. Practice and rehearse.

During the Interview

1. Do not answer questions when

- District staff, school staff, or parents are not yet informed about the issue

- Student privacy is involved

- There is a disaster or emergency—you must notify family first

- There is a news blackout regarding labor negotiations

- The issue is before the courts

2. Pause before answering each question:

- Take time to collect your thoughts.

- Decide whether you want to answer this question. (Does it deal directly with you or your school?)

- Determine whether there is a way you can use your key messages to answer this question.

- Consider a reply using your own words, not those of the reporter.

Key Messages

What do people remember?
What do they tell others?
What appears in the story?

3. Use key messages:

- You need to create a balance between the reporter's goal (to get the information needed to prepare a story) and your goal (to represent your school and get your key messages out).

- Prepare three key messages.

- Use simple words.

- Have an interesting, different, unique point of view.

- Use catchy phrases or words (if appropriate).

- Support key messages with clear, concise examples.

- Insert your key messages into the interview; don't push them.

Send a personalized thank you note to the reporter when your school is highlighted.

 Media Interview Do's and Don'ts

Do:

1. Prepare key messages in advance; know your story; practice.

2. Treat each interview as special, as an opportunity.

3. Respect a reporter's deadline.

4. Be responsive; be honest; be yourself.

5. Stay calm.

6. Stick to your messages and keep it simple.

7. Stick to the agreed-on time and location.

8. Provide additional background information.

9. Leave your business card.

10. Mention the name of your school if it is a good news story.

Don't:

1. Use jargon or acronyms.

2. Guess, speculate, or comment on rumors.

3. Answer hypothetical questions.

4. Say "no comment."

5. Speak "off the record."

6. Let a reporter put words in your mouth.

7. Speak on behalf of others.

8. Express a personal view.

Create a Positive First Impression

You only have one chance to make a first impression; make the most of it.

The Voice of Experience

Managing Conflict and Difficult People

7

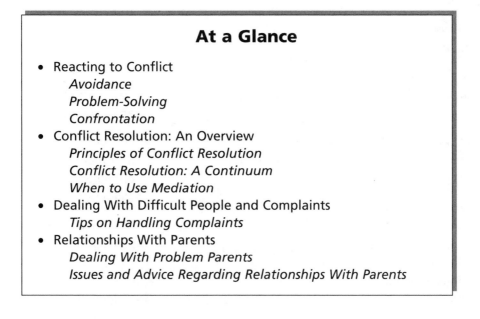

At a Glance

- Reacting to Conflict
  - *Avoidance*
  - *Problem-Solving*
  - *Confrontation*
- Conflict Resolution: An Overview
  - *Principles of Conflict Resolution*
  - *Conflict Resolution: A Continuum*
  - *When to Use Mediation*
- Dealing With Difficult People and Complaints
  - *Tips on Handling Complaints*
- Relationships With Parents
  - *Dealing With Problem Parents*
  - *Issues and Advice Regarding Relationships With Parents*

REACTING TO CONFLICT

Reaction to conflict falls into three basic categories:

> Avoidance
>
> Problem-solving
>
> Confrontation

When dealing with conflict, it can be helpful to notice how the parties are reacting to the situation, whether it's students, staff, parents, or others. It is also useful to monitor your own reaction to conflict in a variety of circumstances. A problem-solving approach has the best results.

 The chart below can be used as an informal checklist to gauge your own reactions.

Avoidance	**Problem-Solving**	**Confrontation**
has a tendency to	has a tendency to	has a tendency to
• allow self to be interrupted, subordinated, stereotyped;	• state feelings, needs, and wants directly;	• interrupt, subordinate, and stereotype others;
• have poor eye contact;	• have good eye contact;	• have intense and glaring eye contact;
• have poor posture and defeated air;	• have straight posture and a competent air;	• have invading posture and an arrogant air;
• withhold information, opinions, and feelings;	• be able to disclose information, opinions, and feelings;	• conceal information, opinions, and feelings;
• be an ineffective listener;	• be an effective listener;	• be an ineffective listener;
• be indecisive;	• initiate and take clear positions;	• dominate;
• apologize, avoid, and leave.	• approach with skill.	• be loud, abusive, blaming, and sarcastic.

⊙ CONFLICT RESOLUTION: AN OVERVIEW

Principles of Conflict Resolution

1. Look for solutions . . . not for blame.

2. Focus on the problem . . . not on the person.

3. Take a nonadversarial approach . . . not an adversarial one.

4. Use dialogue . . . not debate.

5. Focus on interests . . . not on position.

6. Try for a win/win solution . . . not a win/lose one.

7. Focus on change . . . not on control.

8. Conflict resolution is a long process . . . not a quick fix.

Conflict Resolution: A Continuum

Approaches to conflict resolution range from negotiation, to conciliation, to mediation, to arbitration, to litigation.

	Negotiation	*Conciliation*	*Mediation*	*Arbitration*	*Litigation*
Disputants speak to	each other	each other	mediator/ each other	arbitrator	lawyer/ judge
Decision is made by	disputants	disputants	disputants	arbitrator	judge

In **negotiation**, the disputant is most

- responsible for the outcome of the process;
- concerned with the relationship and solving the problem;
- empowered to resolve the conflict.

In **litigation**, the disputant is least

- responsible for the outcome of the process;
- concerned with the relationship and solving the problem;
- empowered to resolve the conflict.

Always follow your district school board's policies and procedures regarding conflict resolution.

If the dispute involves your school advisory group, follow the dispute resolution process set out in your school advisory group bylaws.

When to Use Mediation

Principals may find themselves mediating disputes among a variety of stakeholders in the school community.

Do proceed to mediate if

1. the conflict is specific;

2. both parties perceive you to be neutral;

3. both parties have voluntarily agreed to try mediation;

4. not dealing with the conflict is unacceptable to both disputants;

5. adequate time and space are available.

Do not proceed if

1. the matter includes police involvement or any legal ramifications;

2. the case involves any form of harassment;

3. the matter is the subject of a formal union grievance;

4. the two sides are manifestly unequal;

5. you are in doubt about your own competency or expertise.

Principled or Interest-Based Negotiation: Ten Tips

1. Separate the people from the problem.

2. Focus attention on interests, not positions.

3. Invent alternate options for mutual gain.

4. Base outcomes on objective standards and criteria.

5. Never yield to pressure, only to principle.

6. Don't attack positions; look behind them.

7. Don't defend ideas; ask for criticism and improvements.

8. In the face of personal attacks, rephrase the problem.

9. Ask questions.

10. Use silence.

DEALING WITH DIFFICULT PEOPLE AND COMPLAINTS

Tips on Handling Complaints

Pay Attention   Take all complaints seriously. Don't let small concerns become big ones.

Document	Document each complaint. Record the time and date of the call, and make notes of what was said. File your documentation.
Listen	Practice active listening. Rephrase what you've heard to verify understanding. Ask for further clarification if needed.
	Try to determine if there are underlying issues involved, or just the specific incident that is being reported. Listen to the caller's feelings and ideas.
	See Chapter 5, "Communication," for further tips regarding active listening.
Investigate	Get all the facts from the caller.
	Check out the facts with all parties involved before responding.
Respond	No complaint should go more than a day without a response. Promise to look into the matter and get back to the caller at a specified time.
	Don't make hasty promises that you cannot keep.
	Refer the caller to the appropriate person. For example, when parents have a concern regarding the classroom, arrange for them to speak with the teacher if they have not already done so.
Avoid	Avoid becoming defensive. Don't fabricate excuses.
	Avoid the use of inappropriate language, even if the caller uses such language. If nothing else, agree to disagree. Remain polite and professional; stay calm.
	If the caller becomes abusive and does not respond to your appeal for reason, discontinue the call.

RELATIONSHIPS WITH PARENTS

⊛ Dealing With Problem Parents

1. Communicate

Deal with the issue immediately.

Communicating in a consistent and efficient manner allows the parent to feel that concerns are addressed meaningfully.

Listen for both the immediate concern and the underlying issues.

2. Consider

Possible references to consult include:

- the school's code of conduct,
- the school's bylaw regarding conflict resolution (if the matter involves members of the school advisory group),
- district policies and procedures regarding harassment, conflict resolution, safe schools, and related topics.

3. Respond

Occasionally, parents become confrontational and hostile when they believe that their issue, complaint, or child is not being dealt with appropriately. There are a number of strategies and legal tools that may be used to deal with the problem of parental harassment. The difficulty is determining when such tactics are necessary and which tactic is appropriate in the circumstances.

TIPS

If you feel you are dealing with a problem parent:

- Contact your superintendent.
- Call your professional association.

Issues and Advice Regarding Relationships With Parents

CAUTION: Legal options should be used only after nonlegal strategies have been tried and have failed. Your supervisor should be notified that you wish to pursue legal action. Districts are normally prepared to support principals or vice-principals in taking such action. Consultation with your professional association is also recommended.

1. Issue: What should a principal do when confronted with a parent who is being physically violent or threatening physical violence against him or her?

TIPS *Advice*

Contact the police to lay a charge of assault or uttering threats.

Seek a restraining order to keep the parent away from the administrator at school and at home.

Issue a trespass letter to the parent in the format adopted by your district.

Restrict the parent's access to the school in accordance with your district school board's policy.

2. Issue: What should a principal do when a parent disrupts the school by persistently coming onto school property to confront the administrator, teachers, or other staff?

 Advice

It is recommended that you seek the support of your supervisor for any decision to keep a parent from coming onto school premises and refer to your district school board policy on access to the premises.

3. Issue: A parent publishes or communicates false and defamatory information about an administrator by way of letters to the media, other parents, or the district school board; by circulating petitions or vocalizing statements to other parents at school advisory group meetings or at other public events; or by simply spreading rumors.

 Advice

Seek legal advice through your supervisor, from your district's attorney and your professional association.

Consider starting an action for defamation if the three elements of defamation can be proven and the parent's conduct is malicious.

Where the comments made by the parent are protected by qualified privilege, consider responding to the allegations in a proportionate manner (i.e., to the same audience and using the same means of communication).

4. Issue: A parent repeatedly follows the administrator from place to place, communicates with the administrator or the administrator's family, watches or attends at the administrator's home or school, or engages in threatening conduct.

 Advice

Seek legal advice from your district attorney and your professional association.

Consider sending the parent a "cease and desist" letter.

Contact the police to lay a charge of criminal harassment.

If the police are uncooperative or the parent's conduct does not amount to criminal harassment, consider commencing a civil action, so as to bring a motion for an injunction to restrain the parent from engaging in the harassing behavior.

Relationships With Parents: An Ounce of Prevention Is Worth a Pound of Cure

Be proactive.

Encourage healthy dissent and constructive criticism.

Recognize warning signs of potential problems.

Highlight expectations for parent conduct with particular reference to the purposes of the code of conduct.

Work with senior district administration to develop a districtwide protocol for dealing with problem parents.

Suggested Reading Regarding Relationships With Parents

Carroll, D. P. (1999) When Reasonable Fails: How to Deal With Parents Who Harass School Administrators. *OPC Register*

Keel, R. (2004) Managing Parental and Intruder Harassment. *OPC Register*

Roher, E. M., and Wormwell, S. (2002) "Dealing with the Problem Parent," Chapter 5 in *An Educator's Guide to the Role of the Principal*

Whitaker, T., and Fiore, D. J. (2001) *Dealing With Difficult Parents (and With Parents in Difficult Situations)*

Whitaker, T. (1999) *Dealing with Difficult Teachers*

Take Care to Communicate Effectively With Parents

The one thing that seems to keep things running smoothly is information provided to parents in a timely fashion. Even if the news is not good, parents and guardians need to hear it.

Learn how to have positive and effective communication with parents. Dealing with parents is without doubt the most stressful part of the job.

Fight the urge to interrupt angry parents when they say something that's not true or not grounded. Be patient; wait and listen before you start correcting or setting the facts straight. Even if the parents still disagree with you, they will feel like you've listened.

The Voice of Experience

Effective Meetings

8

At a Glance

- Before the Meeting
  - *Meeting Planning Checklist*
  - *Sample Meeting Agendas*
- During the Meeting
  - *How to Run Effective Meetings: Tips for the Chair*
- After the Meeting

Prepare thoroughly for every meeting you have. To run effective meetings, consider what must be done:

1. Before the meeting (planning)

2. During the meeting (conducting)

3. After the meeting (following up)

BEFORE THE MEETING

1. Consider Two Key Questions

- What is the objective of the meeting?

- Do we really need to have this meeting?

If the answer to the second question is yes, start planning.

2. Plan the Agenda

- Consult the "Meeting Planning Checklist" below.

- Notify participants well in advance of the time, location, and purpose of the meeting.

- Consult with participants for agenda items.

- Carefully consider the order in which you place the items.

- Consider whether purely informative items can be communicated by memo or e-mail instead.

- Distribute the agenda in advance of the meeting.

- Ensure that meeting dates and contents conform to collective agreement requirements.

3. Do Your Homework

- Collect and organize reference materials for the meeting.

- Prepare handouts and audiovisual presentations (e.g., PowerPoint).

- Before the meeting, speak with any individuals who have a vested interest in any agenda items. (For example, teachers should not hear about changes to their teaching assignments for the first time in a full staff meeting.)

- Alert individuals who are required to speak to an item on the agenda.

✓ Meeting Planning Checklist

1. Meeting	Date
	Starting Time
	Ending Time
	Location
2. Participants	Number of participants
	List of participants' names
	Individual name tags
	Name cards for tables
3. Facilities	Accessibility to persons with disabilities
	Appropriate room size

Adequate lighting/heating/cooling/ventilation
Seating: Chevron
U-shaped
Classroom
Round table
Open circle or square
Extra chairs for guests
Tables for participants to write on
Signs directing guests to meeting room

4. Refreshments Tea, coffee, juice, bottled water
Snack food (e.g., muffins)

5. Equipment Laptop
Microphone
Overhead projector
Data projector
Slide projector
Television and VCR

6. Supplies Extension cords
Extra bulbs
Extra copies of the agenda and previous minutes
Flip charts
Handouts
Markers
Masking tape
Overhead pens
Paper and pens
Transparencies

Sample Meeting Agendas

1. Parliamentary Procedure: Order of Business

Roll call of members present

Reading of minutes of last meeting

Officers' reports

Committee reports

Special orders: important business previously designated for consideration at this meeting

Unfinished business

New business

Announcements

Adjournment

2. School Advisory Group Meeting Agenda

Welcome and introductions (15 minutes)

Business arising from the minutes (5 minutes)

Old business and updates (10 minutes)

New business (45 minutes in total)

Principal's report (20 minutes)

Other reports (45 minutes in total)

General information, updates, inquiries (maximum 5 minutes)

Next meeting: date, time, location

Agenda items for next meeting

Adjournment

3. Agenda for Brief or Informal Meetings

When	Meeting date	
	Starting time	
	Ending time	
Where	Location	
Why	Purpose of meeting	
Who	Person who called meeting	
	Names of meeting participants	
What	Agenda items	Time allocated

1. _____ _____ minutes

2. _____ _____ minutes

3. _____ _____ minutes

Stand-Up Meetings

For very brief meetings, consider calling a "stand-up" staff meeting. A stand-up meeting saves time settling in.

It clearly signals that the meeting is designed to pass along information, not to engage in discussion or decision-making.

Wait until everyone has assembled before making your announcements.

4. Staff Meetings: Two Sample Agendas

Sample # 1   **Staff Meeting Agenda**
                      Monday, February 24, 2003
                      3:30 P.M.–5:00 P.M.
                      Library

Refreshments

1. Welcome and introductions (new staff and student teachers)

2. Guest speaker: youth intervention coordinator, police services

3. Debriefing regarding lockdown drill on Feb. 20

4. Staff training regarding report cards

5. Administrivia (2 minutes)

Some principals find it helpful to divide staff meeting agenda items into three categories:

For decision   For discussion   For information

Items can then be placed in order of priority on the agenda and time allocated accordingly.

Sample # 2   **Staff Meeting Agenda**
                      Tuesday, February 25, 2003
                      8:00 A.M.–9:00 A.M.
                      Staff Room

Coffee and donuts available starting at 7:45 A.M.

1. Welcome and introductory remarks

2. Information items and announcements (See items posted on staff intranet.)

3. Items for discussion and decision

4. Professional development:

The Written Curriculum, the Taught Curriculum, and the Tested Curriculum: a presentation by staff members who attended the recent conference.

5. Committee reports:

   School advisory group Information and Communication Technology Committee

6. Items of new business (added here at start of meeting; to be discussed or deferred to next meeting)

7. Dates to note: see attached calendar for March

8. Adjournment: 9:00 A.M.

Next full-staff meeting: Tuesday, March 25, 8:00 A.M.–9:00 A.M.

DURING THE MEETING

Before the meeting starts, check that the equipment is working.

If the group meets regularly, establish a meeting schedule for the year. Otherwise, set the next meeting date at the end of each meeting.

TIPS **How to Run Effective Meetings: Tips for the Chair**

Opening

Start and end the meeting on time.

Keep opening remarks welcoming but brief.

Introduce any guests.

Review the agenda. Keep to the agenda and the timelines.

Conducting

If new business items are raised and there is not time for them, note them and carry them forward to the next meeting.

Maintain order and focus. Discuss one piece of business at a time.

Do not allow discussions that breach privacy.

Participating

Allow for individual and small group input during discussion items. Try to involve all participants.

Remain neutral and provide alternative ways to solve problems or make decisions.

Encourage decision-making through consensus.

Formalize decisions through rules of order, if desired.

Closing

Summarize the meeting, reviewing key actions and decisions.

Check that all participants have the same understanding of any decisions.

Review the time, date, and location of the next meeting and any items of new business that will be included on the next agenda.

Ensure that the meeting room is cleaned and restored to its original condition.

Establishing Norms for the Meeting

At the beginning of the meeting, use consensus to establish the norms for the meeting.

This may not be necessary every time you meet if you have a regular group of participants who clearly understand and agree upon the norms for the meeting.

However, if it is the first time the group has met, if the circumstances have changed, or if the group has new members or observers, take time at the beginning of the meeting to establish the norms for behavior and decision-making.

AFTER THE MEETING

Ensure that minutes are written and distributed to all participants and to those members who were unable to attend.

Keep commitments you made during the meeting to take certain actions or to find particular information and pass it along.

Send thank you notes to those who made a presentation or an extra contribution toward the success of the meeting.

Begin the process of planning for the next meeting.

From time to time, seek input from group members regarding the effectiveness of the meetings. Ask for suggestions for improvement and implement those that are feasible.

Meetings at a Distance: Using Technology to Save Time and Money

Some meetings can be held successfully at a distance, using any one of three different approaches: audio conference calls, video conferencing, or Web conferencing.

Meetings at a distance save participants the time and expense of traveling to a meeting site.

Once a face-to-face relationship has been established among participants, electronic meetings can be quite effective.

Start by asking yourself two questions:

1. What is the objective of the meeting?

2. Do we really need to have this meeting?

To have a successful meeting at a distance, you must follow all the traditional steps for planning an effective meeting.

Meeting correspondence (notice of meeting, agenda, minutes) can be handled electronically.

Consider carefully the purpose of your meeting before deciding to meet at a distance rather than in person.

Resources for Effective Meetings

Educational publications and Web sites will have information on running effective meetings.

Preparing for and running meetings includes the topics below.
> Meeting room organizer checklist
> Creating an agenda
> Keeping minutes of school advisory group meetings
> A sample school advisory group agenda
> A sample of minutes
> Tips for reaching decisions by consensus
> Decisions made by voting, including how to make, amend, and withdraw motions
> Effective meeting strategies
> The role of the chair

Keep Your Sense of Humor

Have a sense of humor. Laugh a lot, especially at yourself.

Don't take anything too personally; it's not about you.

The Voice of Experience

Records and Information Management

GETTING STARTED

One administrative duty you must become familiar with is records and information management. *Records* include information about pupils and required reports that are kept at the school. *Information management* involves the organization of both paper and electronic files.

1. When you review records management, ensure that you have appropriate security and backup systems in place to preserve and protect the privacy of all your electronic records. The district may require that a paper copy be filed of records that were generated electronically (e.g., letters of suspension, expulsion, and trespass).

2. When you organize your own office, follow the existing filing practices at first; take time to determine whether there is any need to alter these procedures at some point in the future. Some principals have filing cabinets in their offices; others ask their administrative assistants to keep all paper files in the general office. Ask the office coordinator and vice-principal to brief you regarding existing procedures used for record and information management.

Follow your district procedures for information management.

3. When you store information, you must do so in such a way that it can be easily accessed when needed; at the same time, access must be restricted to those who have a right to the information.

Maintaining confidentiality of information is the responsibility of every staff member. Ensure that everyone at the school, including itinerant staff, student teachers, and volunteers, handles all personal information with discretion.

Freedom of information and protection of privacy are outlined in legislation, as well as in your district's policies and procedures. Follow your district's procedures regarding how to establish, maintain, retain, transfer, and dispose of pupil records.

TIPS

If records and information management is a priority for you this year, arrange to visit experienced colleagues at other schools to discuss their procedures.

Also, arrange for your office administrator to do the same.

Copying

Familiarize yourself with your district's copy agreement.

Post relevant information near photocopiers and bring it to the attention of staff.

CONFIDENTIALITY AND DISCLOSURE

Student Records and the Courts

Educators are required to maintain confidentiality with respect to the contents of a record that comes to their knowledge in the course of their duties. Parents of a student have access to the student's records if the student is younger than 18 years of age. Parent volunteers at the school and school advisory group members do not have access to information contained in pupil records other than those of their own children.

If you are asked to produce in court the records of a current or former student, seek legal advice through your supervisor or from your district's lawyer regarding disclosure and court procedures. Contact your professional association. If it is determined that you should provide records to the court, take the original and a photocopy with you and request that the copy be submitted. If the production of school records is directed by a subpoena or summons, produce only those records expressly demanded by the court document and only if and when directed to do so by the judge.

Follow your district's procedures regarding student records.

Confidential Information and the Courts

Principals, teachers, and other school professionals (e.g., social workers) often have information communicated to them in confidence by students. Education-related and child protection legislation imposes specific duties of confidentiality on educators. In addition, various professional codes of ethics provide guidance regarding confidentiality matters for teachers, counselors, social workers, and psychologists, among others. Concomitant with the duty to maintain student confidentiality is the equally important and at times supervening duty of disclosure in certain circumstances as prescribed by legislation. The issue of disclosure of information imparted in confidence is sensitive and complex.

If you are required to attend court for any reason, seek prior legal advice through your supervisor or from the district's lawyer, and contact your local professional association for advice and assistance. If you believe you may be asked to disclose confidential information by the court, discuss this with the district lawyer and your professional association in advance.

Confidentiality and the Duty to Report

The law in most jurisdictions makes it clear that educators have a duty to report to the appropriate child protection agency if they have reason to suspect (or information regarding) a child who is or may be in need of protection. This applies even though the information may be confidential or privileged. Follow your district's procedures regarding reporting suspected child abuse and neglect. See Chapter 23, "Protecting Our Students," for further information.

STUDENT RECORDS

It is the duty of the principal of a school to

1. Establish, maintain, retain, transfer, and dispose of a record for each student enrolled in the school in compliance with the policies established by the district school board

2. Ensure that the materials in the student records are collected and stored in accordance with the policies established by the district school board

3. Ensure the security of the student records

4. Ensure that all persons specified by a district to perform clerical functions with respect to the establishment and maintenance of the student records are aware of the confidentiality provisions in the Education Act and the relevant freedom of information and protection of privacy legislation

Follow your district's procedures regarding student records.

Handling Student Records

Each time you handle a student record, for whatever reason, review its contents and organization. In this way you are conducting your own informal audit of the student records in the school. At the same time, you are learning more about the students and also about the staff members who have prepared the documents in the student records.

Student Records and Record Keeping Regarding Violent Incidents

Follow your district's procedures as well as any relevant legislation regarding record keeping and violent incidents.

Develop the Documentation Habit

TIPS

Written records must be specific; note the date, time, place, and people involved.

Take care to be accurate, factual, and objective.

The documentation is not complete until it's filed.

LEGISLATION REGARDING RECORDS AND INFORMATION MANAGEMENT

Several pieces of legislation (and guidelines) have an impact on records and information management in the school. Consult your district policy and procedures and seek advice from your professional association to ensure you are familiar with and following these policies and procedures.

Management of Confidential Information

In many jurisdictions, confidential information about young offenders may be disclosed to school representatives by police or court officers where the disclosure is necessary to ensure compliance of the young person with a court order, or to ensure the safety of staff, students, or other persons. In turn, the school representatives receiving this information may not disclose the information to any other person unless that disclosure is necessary to ensure that the young person complies with a court order, or to ensure the safety of staff, students, or other persons. The information must usually be kept separate from any other school record of the young person and should be destroyed when no longer needed for the reason it was disclosed.

The Freedom of Information and Protection of Privacy Act

The Freedom of Information and Protection of Privacy Act exists to

- provide a right of access to information under the control of institutions;

- protect the privacy of individuals with respect to personal information held by institutions; and

- provide individuals with a right of access to that information.

Follow your district's procedures regarding freedom of information and protection of privacy.

TIPS

Access and Privacy in the School System

Follow your district's procedures concerning the public display of photos of students, student work with names attached, etc. Obtain appropriate written consent in advance. Consult your school district Web site for access and privacy guidelines in your school district.

A sample Web site for relevant FAQs is www.ipc.on.ca. On this Web site you will find 10 relevant FAQ (Frequently Asked Questions) Fact Sheets:

1. Collection of personal information by a school or school district

2. Correction of personal information

3. School photographs

4. School yearbooks

5. Health card numbers

6. Separated spouses

7. Trustee records

8. Confidential reports

9. Information requested from a school or a school district

10. Police services

Child and Family Services Information

It is imperative that you discharge your legislative duties as well as following your district's procedures regarding reporting suspected child abuse and neglect. Not only could a failure to do so bring harm to a child, it might also expose you to employment sanctions and professional discipline. A report can be made to a child protection agency by telephone or in writing. Keep a record of conversations with the agency, including the name of the worker, the date and time of the call, and the decision of whether the matter will be investigated. In the course of making the report, you must disclose all necessary identifying information concerning the student so that the child protection agency can fully investigate and take whatever steps it deems necessary in accordance with its mandate. Pay close attention to whether relevant legislation or district policy *require* that you inform (or not inform) the student's parent(s) or guardian(s) before making the report. The duty to report will almost always supervene any duty of confidentiality.

Most often, the legislative duty to report will include the following three principles:

Duty to report child in need of protection: If a person, including a person who performs professional or official duties with respect to children, has reasonable grounds to suspect abuse, the person must report the suspicion and the information on which it is based to an agency.

Ongoing duty to report: A person who has additional, reasonable grounds to suspect abuse must make a further report even if he or she has made previous reports with respect to the same child.

Person must report directly: A person who has a duty to report abuse must make the report directly to the agency and shall not rely on any other person to report on his or her behalf.

To shred or not to shred? That is the question.

It's difficult to generalize about what to shred or not to shred.

If you are disposing of confidential information, shred it—do not put it in the recycle basket.

If you have items in a student record that are no longer conducive to the improvement of instruction, shred them, provided they do not need to be retained.

The special-needs identification process generates many documents and copies; shred copies of reports and documents once the originals have been filed.

If you have items in personnel files that are no longer required, shred them. Check your district's human resources policies and procedures for guidelines concerning the retention of employee records.

Handwritten notes that have been transferred to electronic or hard copy can be shredded.

If you are in doubt, ask your superintendent of schools or other district staff.

Make Decisions Wisely

Don't be afraid to say, "I don't know."

Don't always feel that you have to have an answer on the spot. Especially in tight situations that are sensitive or political, buy yourself time. Say to the parent or individual, "Let me look into that and gather the necessary information. I'll get back to you."

The Voice of Experience

Budget and Resource Management

⊚ SCHOOL BUDGET: AN OVERVIEW

Among the many responsibilities associated with the role of the principal is the financial management of the school. This chapter will assist you in understanding your role in the financial procedures and point you in the right direction as you contemplate decisions regarding school budgets, spending, and controls.

Education legislation spells out the financial responsibilities of the principal. In addition, the local district will have certain policies and procedures in place to enforce and clarify the intent of the legislation. These can be sorted into two groups: local financial responsibility and districtwide impact. These groups and the related issues are detailed below.

Most districts will have comprehensive documentation on all these issues in the form of reference material, policy and procedure manuals, and legislation, in a written manual or on a district Web site. It is especially important for newly appointed principals and vice-principals to become familiar with these documents.

This chapter attempts to recognize the large disparity between districts and schools in terms of what is practical, while at the same time highlighting key elements of control. It is not intended to conflict with your own district's policies and procedures, which are paramount. When in doubt, contact your district office.

Education and Budgets

While there may be no specific mention of financial responsibilities in legislation or in district manuals, there may be a reference to reporting and the organization and management of the school through the supervisory officer. Implied in that is the financial management of school-based activities, which will be elaborated on further in the local district policies and procedures.

Conflict of Interest

A conflict of interest may arise where a person in authority is involved in an activity that can result in personal gain to himself or herself, to a family member, or to a close associate. An example could involve the purchase of school materials from a relative, without involving the open competitive purchasing process. Another example would be a purchase for the school, made from a company that the person in authority owns or has an interest in. This can have serious consequences for the employee. When in doubt, check with your district business office.

LOCAL FINANCIAL RESPONSIBILITY (PROTECTING YOURSELF)

Principals have control over the school funds allocated from the overall district budget, as well as supplementary funds raised locally. It is their responsibility to ensure that funds are controlled and used appropriately.

Purchasing Procedures

Generally speaking, schools should not go out and buy items directly, unless they are small purchases in which petty cash can be used. Districts have purchasing departments whose role it is to obtain the best pricing through bulk buying, through an open competitive process that is fair to the taxpayers and that ensures that certain standards are maintained. This is usually achieved through the issuance of a purchase order. (Refer also to sections on conflict of interest and purchasing policy.)

Transparency and Accountability

These are two key concepts to keep in mind when developing and managing your school budget.

TIPS

School Budget

School budget refers to the portion of the district budget that is distributed to the school for the purchase of classroom and office supplies and services. The degree to which the budget is allocated to the school or controlled centrally is up to each district. In one extreme, it could include staff salaries and maintenance of the building, which would be a complete cost center model. More common is the distribution of a budget allocation for discretionary items, such as the following:

- Photocopying

- Equipment rental

- Textbooks

- Telephone

- Admission fees

- Furniture and equipment

- Professional development

- Temporary help

It is the principal's responsibility to stay within the school's budget. He or she may allocate amounts to each department or control it all in the principal's office, but the bottom line is that a principal must stay within the total allocation.

Most districts provide their schools with monthly financial reports to help them monitor their spending. Some districts offer daily access online. Depending on the system in their district, some schools keep a supplementary file of expenses to balance the district's books. This practice of keeping two sets of books can create redundancies and duplication. In any event, it is the schools' responsibility to monitor their spending within the guidelines from the district.

TIPS

> **Your number one criterion for decision-making when allocating funds and resources is the impact on student learning.**
>
> Is this decision in the best interest of the students?
>
> Is this decision aligned with our current priorities?

Petty Cash

Petty cash provides a small sum of money to schools allowing them to buy small items directly rather than through the district's purchasing department. Depending on the district and the size of the school, funds may range from a few hundred dollars to a few thousand. The funds are charged against the school budget.

A bank account requiring two signatures and held jointly in the name of the district and the school is recommended, rather than leaving cash in a drawer. There is a requirement for monthly bank statements (not a passbook), supporting receipts, and regular bank reconciliations to satisfy the district that the funds are being controlled properly.

This fund must not be used to provide loans to staff and should be kept separate from any nondistrict funds as described below. Consult your district business office for guidance.

Depending on the size of the fund, a manual set of books may be appropriate, similar to those you use to balance your personal budget at home. For larger amounts, you may want to investigate the use of a small software accounting package. Due to the cash issue, tight controls are a requirement and the fund is subject to an audit. It is important to monitor and balance this fund on a regular basis.

As a supplement to petty cash, some districts use credit cards for small purchases. These purchase cards work like a personal Visa or MasterCard and are charged to the school budget. Controls over usage and safeguarding of the card(s) are the responsibility of the principal.

Expense Reimbursement

Reimbursement for items such as mileage requires proper documentation and timely submission, at least on a quarterly basis, to ensure that it is charged to the correct budget year.

Nondistrict Funds (Nonpublic Funds)

Nondistrict funds are those raised or collected from sources other than the operating or capital budgets of the district. Control of nondistrict funds (also known as nonpublic funds, or fundraising) is an area of much discussion as to who has responsibility and authority and what level of reporting detail is required. Depending on the school's geographic area (urban or rural), community involvement, etc., the fundraising activities may be modest or substantial. It is important to spell out the purpose, intended disposition, and time frame for the fundraising activity before it takes place to avoid any disagreements down the road.

There are two general categories of nondistrict funds, and different groups are responsible for ensuring that they are used as intended. Local district policy should further clarify the expectations and responsibilities of each group.

School Administered

School administered nondistrict funds are, for example, funds raised for student council activities, field trips, or special events. They are under the direct responsibility and authority of the principal. Since the principal is responsible to a supervisor and the district, there is an implied central responsibility to ensure that the funds are collected and expended appropriately and within district school board policy. Certain basic controls are recommended, including

- a bank account separate from petty cash,

- a requirement for two signatures on the checks,

- bank reconciliations,

- a proper filing of source documents.

The bookkeeping system can parallel that of petty cash. Usually a volunteer looks after this account, but financial controls should be maintained, and where funds are raised for a specific purpose there is an obligation to ensure that they are expended for that purpose.

An annual report should be submitted to the district business office. Depending on the district, it may be subject to audit.

Parent Administered

Parent administered nondistrict funds could be, for example, those of the school advisory group, the parent teacher association, or the home and school association. *Parent administered* implies that the parent group has sole signing authority on the account. All fundraising must adhere to district policy and regulation.

If the principal is a signing officer, however, then these funds belong in the school administered category above and are under more direct control of the district school board.

Audit

All financial activity of the school is subject to audit on a random, scheduled, or targeted basis and either internally by board business staff or externally by the district auditor. As a result, it is important to ensure that proper procedures and record keeping are maintained.

Insurance

The school district has property insurance coverage for the school building and liability insurance for potential issues related to staff, students, and visitors. It is the principal's responsibility to inspect the building on a regular basis and to report deterioration or safety matters. Injury or threat of lawsuits should be communicated immediately to the appropriate district departments to ensure proper coverage and response. Lawsuits can implicate those indirectly responsible (principal, school district) as well as those perceived to be directly responsible.

Asset Control

The principal is responsible for the safekeeping of the assets of the school, including the following:

- Furniture

- Equipment

- Computers

- Athletic equipment

- Musical instruments

It is recommended that schools maintain an inventory of these assets to assist in any insurance claims and to help the teaching staff monitor the equipment under their direct control. Assets that are deemed surplus to the school should be reported to the district business office to ensure appropriate reallocation or disposal.

Transfer of School Principal

It is important when a principal transfers from one school to another, or retires, that he or she leaves the school in good financial order for the new principal, including a reconciled bank account and budget surplus position. This includes the transfer of signing authorities on any school bank account(s). The "Do unto others" adage applies; you would not want to inherit a school with financial problems.

> Principals must follow district school board direction faithfully and seek assistance whenever necessary.
>
> Caution should be the watchword when it comes to financial management.

BOARDWIDE IMPACT (PROTECTING THE DISTRICT SCHOOL BOARD)

Over and above the control of the local school budget, principals, as agents of the board, can also impact the overall operations that may result in the application of financial penalties or inefficiencies beyond the school and on the overall district.

Purchasing Policy

The policy spells out the authority of the purchasing department, schools, and departments with respect to the competitive process and thresholds. It is especially important in a public organization funded by the taxpayer to ensure that there are equal opportunities for companies to bid and obtain contracts from the district for the provision of goods and services, in addition to securing the best pricing.

Hiring Part-Time Staff

Human resources departments determine who is an employee and is therefore subject to income tax and other statutory deductions. This can only be determined, and payment can only be remitted, centrally through the payroll department. If a school engages and pays an individual without going through the proper human resource department process and the district does not remit the appropriate taxes, the district can be subject to financial penalties.

Contracts

A contract with an individual or company is legally binding. Contracts therefore should be controlled and authorized centrally through the district business office and not through the school. Sales representatives who attempt to negotiate a contract directly with the school should be referred to the district purchasing department. Considerations include the following:

- Length of contract

- Terms and penalties

- Board standards

It is important to note that a contract stays with the school; therefore, if a principal is transferred, the new principal is bound by the existing contract that may limit his or her options for the future.

Technology

Technology is exciting, and it can be difficult to resist the bargain at the local electronics store if you have sufficient funds in your budget. Stop!

Technology is probably the third largest portion of the district budget after salaries and building maintenance. Adherence to districtwide standards of hardware, software, and network is critical. Stores always have weekly specials, and on a given day their price may seem lower than the district-negotiated price. You must look beyond the shelf price. The district contract probably includes items such as multiyear warranty, software loading, network standards, and possibly training. Impulse purchases can cause additional expense to the district as a whole and may not be supportable by your information technology department.

Enrollment Reporting

Enrollment reporting drives the funding that establishes the budget for the district and the school allocation and staffing. It is therefore critical for schools to be as accurate as possible in their student average daily enrollment count. These counts are subject to audit.

Funding Model

Principals should be familiar with the structure of the state funding model to better understand the budget constraints faced by the district and to be in a position to convey the right message to staff and community members.

 ## TIPS REGARDING BUDGET AND RESOURCE MANAGEMENT

1. Monitor your substitute teacher budget closely, if it is assigned to the school. Inform your supervisor if you have concerns that it will not last the year.

- Follow district policy to distribute and track any professional development funds for staff.

- Monitor the photocopier budget closely; it can get away on you quickly.

- Add an appropriate percentage to every purchase order to cover applicable taxes as well as shipping and handling costs; this eliminates nasty surprises when the invoice arrives.

2. Find out if building maintenance is a school budget item. Determine what you must fund; for example, you need to know who pays for the soap in the washrooms and the salt for the icy parking lot. Find out how major repairs (e.g., roof repairs) are funded.

3. Apprise yourself of additional sources of district funds and how to access them. For example:

- A superintendent's contingency fund

- Centrally held special education funds

- Funds accessible through proposals submitted by individual schools
- Professional development funds
- Funds for replacement of furniture and equipment
- Funds earmarked for computer hardware or software acquisitions
- Funds earmarked for learning resources to support the curriculum

4. Follow district policy regarding nonpublic funds. All fundraising must adhere to district policy, whether it is school or parent administered. Follow your district's procedures regarding accounting for nonpublic funds; they may be audited.

   a. Cash and checks collected by the school from students and staff for

- sales of chocolate bars and gym uniforms,
- walk-a-thons and read-a-thons,
- band concerts and dances
- athletic fees,
- collections from students and parents for field trips,
- vending machine sales and proceeds from cafeteria operations,
- student fees and school photo rebates,
- donations received from school advisory group.

   b. School-generated funds raised through fundraising that is

- school administered (under the direct control of the principal) or
- parent administered (where the parent group has sole signing authority)

5. Find out if

- student fees are charged (if so, review the fee to ensure it conforms to district policy),
- there are any other nondistrict funds available in the school,
- the school is involved in any partnerships or cooperative ventures,
- the school is the recipient of any sponsorships or donations.

6. Make effective use of volunteers, student teachers, and co-op students; they support student and staff learning. You may use community

resources to augment school resources. Exercise caution in this regard and be sure to follow district procedures.

7.   Review district policy and ask the office coordinator (and other appropriate staff) to brief you on past practice at the school regarding

- school budgeting and accounting,
- requisitions and purchase orders,
- petty cash and purchase of low-value items,
- bank accounts and signing authority,
- the school safe and combination,
- the use of technology to support resource management and budget processes,
- school credit cards (purchasing cards).

Be sure to get a thorough briefing on this last item. Purchases on the credit cards are charged to the school budget, and the principal is responsible for controls over the usage and safeguarding of the card.

Ensure that practices conform to district policy.

8.   Familiarize yourself with the process for ordering, storing, and distributing

- student consumables—for example, paper and art supplies—and
- staff consumables—for example, staplers and computer disks.

Monitor inventories of consumables as well as furniture and equipment inventories; for example, computers, athletic equipment, musical instruments. Follow district procedures.

9.   Ask the custodian to brief you on all aspects of resource management concerning the physical plant. Encourage and support suggestions from all staff, students, and parents to reduce inefficiencies and maximize cost effectiveness; for example, ways to reduce paper use or fuel consumption.

10. Introduce yourself to central staff at the district office who are responsible for

- school budget accounts,
- purchasing,
- online budget inquiry system,
- school maintenance and repairs.

Do not hesitate to ask central staff for information, advice, and assistance. When in doubt, contact your district office or help desk.

> ## Delegate
>
> Know when to ask for help. Don't believe that if you do it all yourself, then you must be a good administrator.
>
> Hire some temporary office help for the really busy times, if you can. Take time to find and train the right people; this pays off many times over in the future when you need assistance.
>
> Delegate, but don't abdicate.
>
> *The Voice of Experience*

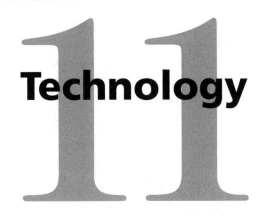

Technology

GETTING STARTED

Using technology effectively is an integral part of almost every aspect of the principal's job. This chapter will provide a brief overview of several technology issues that you may wish to consider as a beginning principal or as a principal new to a school.

Getting Oriented in Your New School

1. Review

Review your district policies and procedures regarding computers, information technology, software, school Web sites, student and staff use of the Internet, and other related issues. Review relevant school policies and procedures and the school's Information and Communication Technology Plan. Are they aligned with district policies?

2. Prepare

Become familiar with your own computer in your new office. Get *all* the passwords you need and keep records of them in a safe place. Change personal passwords as appropriate. If you are new to the e-mail system (e.g., FirstClass Client, GroupWise, Lotus Notes, Outlook), arrange to learn how to use it immediately. (Review "Tips for Communicating by E-Mail" in Chapter 5.) Learn how to use other features of your office computer; for example, scheduling meetings in your electronic calendar, setting the meeting notifier alarm.

Know how to use all aspects of the public address system effectively.

3. Meet

District allocated technology support. Call and introduce yourself before you need to make that first urgent call for help. If you are new to the district, arrange to meet with an experienced principal to discuss technology issues in the local schools.

Office coordinator. Discuss the use of computers and technology in the office. Who is responsible for administrative tasks (e.g., attendance, budget)?

Computer or technology contact teacher. Discuss the use of technology at the school. Identify past successes, current priorities, emerging issues, and future concerns. Ask for a tour with a guided overview of the use of technology in the school.

Familiarize yourself as quickly as possible with the technology in your school as it relates to

- you,

- the staff and the students,

- the parents and the broader community.

✓ Technology Inventory

Review the school's inventory of information and communication technology equipment. Conduct your own informal technology inventory as you do a building walk-through. Inquire about items that you would expect to see but cannot find. Add to the list below as you find other items. These devices range from low-tech telephones to high-tech state-of-the-art scientific equipment.

Communication

Audio conferencing, video conferencing, and Web conferencing capabilities

Cell phones

Desktops

E-mail system

Fax machines

Internet connections

Laptops

Voicemail system

Walkie-talkies

Visual

Digital cameras

Overhead projectors and LCD panels

Televisions

Video cameras

Video monitors for morning announcements

Videocassette recorders (VCRs)

Videodisk players

Organizational

Handheld personal computers and electronic organizers

Technology can be used to assist with school administration, classroom instruction, and group presentations.

→ Further Considerations for Getting Started

Here are some issues for further consideration:

1. The school technology plan
2. Technology and the curriculum
3. Technology and school administration
4. Technology and staff development
5. The acquisition of new information and communication hardware
6. The acquisition of new educational and administrative software
7. The location and use of technological devices
8. The maintenance of equipment
9. The establishment and maintenance of an inventory for hardware and software
10. The safe use of the Internet by students; acceptable use policies for all users

TIPS

Safe Use of the Internet

For further information regarding the safe use of the Internet, see the Web site list later in this chapter.

What is out?	**What is in?**
Wires	Wireless
"Sage on Stage"	Networks of teachers and learners
Computer labs	Ubiquitous technology
Textbooks as dominant medium	Internet as dominant medium
Desktop PCs	Laptops and palmtops

SOURCE: Adapted from *Managing the Transition from Paper to Light*, A. C. November.

TECHNOLOGY AND SCHOOL ADMINISTRATION

Administrative Software

Familiarize yourself with the administrative software used throughout the school for report cards, timetabling, special education documentation, budget, library cataloging, and purchasing. You do not need to be able to personally use every piece of administrative software, but it is helpful to know what software is used, who uses it, and for what purpose. It is also important to determine who the backup person is for a particular task (e.g., daily online reporting of staff absences) in the event that the usual staff member is not available for the job.

Personal Productivity Technology

Make a conscious effort to keep yourself up-to-date on new software and technology that you can use to make your own job easier. Software designed for word processing, accounting, timetabling, personal scheduling, and data management is readily available and constantly updated. Find out what your experienced colleagues recommend, establish your priorities, and identify the new software programs and technologies that you want to master this year.

Assess Your Own Technology Skills

The online version of *The School Administrator* for April 1999 (Johnson and Bartleson, 1999) presents a series of 10 rubrics to determine what school leaders should know and be able to do with information technologies. You can use these rubrics to assess your skill levels and then plan for your own professional development.

1. Personal productivity

2. Information systems use

3. Record keeping and budget

4. Use of data

5. Communications skills

6. Online research

7. Teacher competencies

8. Student competencies

9. Visioning and planning

10. Ethical use and policy making

For further details, visit the American Association of School Administrators Web site at www.aasa.org.

Using the Internet to Assist You With Your Job

Use the Internet to conduct online research and to find specific information that you need to help you carry out your responsibilities. Bookmark your favorite sites and monitor them regularly.

1. Bookmark your district Web site for quick access to policies and procedures.

2. See the list of Web sites in the Resources section at the end of this handbook for additional addresses.

> Check your district policy and procedures regarding acceptable use of computers and Internet or intranet technology and computer network security.

TECHNOLOGY AND THE CURRICULUM

Specific uses of technology are usually incorporated into the mandated curriculum at all grade levels. As a principal, you monitor the integration of technology into the curriculum when you observe the teaching and learning process, oversee student achievement, assess school programs, and evaluate staff performance. Becoming familiar with the instructional software programs used in the school is helpful. When you demonstrate an informed interest in information and communication technology, you encourage its use as a tool to support student and staff learning.

The Role of Technology in the Curriculum: An Overview

- *Information literacy* is the ability to access, select, gather, critically evaluate, create, and communicate information, and to use the information obtained to solve problems and make decisions. In preparation for further education, employment, citizenship, and lifelong learning, students must be capable of deriving meaning from information by using a wide variety of information literacy skills.

- As part of their training in computer and information literacy, students should become familiar with a range of available software programs, simulations, multimedia resources, databases, and computer-assisted learning modules.

- Students will also be expected to use software applications that help them develop general skills in such areas as writing, problem-solving, research, and communication.

- It is important that students learn to critically evaluate the accuracy, validity, currency, comprehensiveness, and depth of the information they access using information technology, particularly the Internet.

- In general, teachers must try to ensure that students acquire the knowledge, skills, and attitudes that will allow them to use computer and information technology safely, effectively, confidently, and ethically.

- As the technology capable of enhancing student learning becomes available, teachers should, within a reasonable period of time, incorporate that technology into their planning of instruction and learning activities in individual disciplines and, collaboratively, across disciplines.

- Effective school library programs can also help to promote the development of information literacy skills among all students by supporting and coordinating the collaborative planning and implementation of reading programs, inquiry and research tasks, and independent study.

BUILDING YOUR SCHOOL TECHNOLOGY PLAN

Once you have familiarized yourself with the current status of information technology in your new school, you will want to begin the process of planning for the future. Remember that a planning process was in place before you arrived, so you will be building on what went before. As in all areas of school improvement planning, you will want to acknowledge the work done to date.

Check your district policies and procedures regarding school technology plans. If your district has a template for school plans, follow it. Beyond that, think outside the box when developing your plan.

 Ten Essential Elements for Developing an Effective Technology Plan

1. Create a vision

2. Involve all stakeholders

3. Gather data

4. Review the research

5. Integrate technology into the curriculum

6. Commit to professional development

7. Ensure a sound infrastructure

8. Allocate appropriate funding and budget

9. Plan for ongoing monitoring and assessment

10. Prepare for tomorrow

SOURCE: Adapted from *Successful K-12 Technology Planning: Ten Essential Elements*, H. Barnett.

TIPS

Remember to delegate when appropriate.

You cannot do everything yourself, nor should you.

→ Building Your School Technology Plan: A Starting Point

As you get under way with your Information and Communication Technology Planning Committee, the following concepts may help stimulate lively discussion and forward thinking:

1. The new education paradigm makes a shift from content-based curriculum to process-based curriculum.

2. The new paradigm focuses on transparent usage of technology rather than on just the tool.

3. The new paradigm focuses on information fluency, critical thinking and problem-solving skills, and real-world communication skills.

4. We must visualize that future, but it is not about technology—it is about the social power of technology to fundamentally transform the world.

5. When these concepts serve as the foundation for the technology plan, the focus will be on how to improve student learning rather than buying the latest technology, such as multimedia equipment, and then trying to figure out what to do with it.

SOURCE (#1–4): *New Schools for the New Age*, I. Jukes and T. McCain.

SOURCE (#5): *The Scourge of Technolust: No More Shopping Lists!* A. C. November.

If you have a technology planning committee, thank them for their contributions to date.

Re-engineer the process to plan for information and communication instead of technology.

Let go of the technocentric focus.

What is out?   Technology Committees

What is in?   Information Communications Committees

　　　　　—Managing the Transition from Paper to Light, A. C. November

Communicate Constantly

Don't be afraid to overcommunicate.

Ask yourself: Who needs to know this? How will I communicate it to them?

When do I need to communicate it?

The Voice of Experience

School
Advisory Groups

➔ **PREPARING TO WORK WITH YOUR SCHOOL ADVISORY GROUP**

> The purpose of the school advisory group is to improve pupil achievement and to enhance the accountability of the education system to parents.

An effective school advisory group can be one of your school's greatest assets. Establishing a positive working relationship with the members is critical to the success of the advisory group.

School advisory groups continue to be advisory in nature. They are entitled to make recommendations to the principal of the school or to the district school board on any matter. Principals (and districts) must receive and consider the recommendations of the school advisory group, but they are not required to accept them. As the principal of the school, you must respond to each group recommendation. You can accept and implement the recommendation, or implement a revised version, or reject the recommendation altogether. You must advise the group of the action you have taken.

Here are some steps to consider, whether you are new to the school or starting a school year with a new advisory group in the same school. Begin by scanning the environment; don't start by jumping in and changing things.

Review Current Legislation and Relevant Documentation

Review any district policies and procedures regulating school advisory groups; for example,

- Community use of schools

- School communications

- Fundraising in schools

- Student Dress Code

- Reimbursement for expenses of school advisory group

- Volunteers

- Accounting for nondistrict funds

Also review the following:

- The school advisory group's constitution and bylaws. If they do not exist, review the constitutions of other schools' groups in order to have samples for consideration. Ensure that a process exists for conflict resolution and expulsion of dysfunctional members.

- The school advisory group's annual report and minutes from last year

- The school advisory group's newsletters from last year and articles in school newsletters

Gather Further Information

If you are new to the school, invite key people to update you on school advisory group issues:

- Vice-principal (note: the vice-principal should attend all advisory group meetings)

- School advisory group chair

- Community representative

- School office administrator

- Custodian

- Teacher representative

- Nonteacher representative

- Student representative (if appropriate)

Set up an initial meeting with the school advisory group chair to get acquainted.

WORKING WITH YOUR SCHOOL ADVISORY GROUP

Getting Under Way

Meet with the school advisory group chair to discuss goals, communication, and other items.

1. **Goals**

    a. Chair

    - Personal views and beliefs

    - List of issues and concerns regarding the school and the group

    b. Principal

- Personal views and beliefs and general goals
- List of issues and concerns regarding the school and the group

    c. Linking group activities and goals to student achievement

2. **Communication**

    a. Between principal and chair and group

- Regular meetings
- Telephone calls
- E-mails

    b. Between principal and community

- Web site
- Newsletters
- Local newspaper

    c. Between school advisory group and school staff

- Group newsletters
- Bulletin board
- Web site

3. **Administrative Items** (Check district policy for these)

- Advisory authority of group
- Composition of group
- Consultation with the district staff
- Consultation with parents of the school community
- Creation of a bylaw establishing a conflict resolution process for internal advisory group disputes and the exclusion of dysfunctional members
- Election of parent members and other members
- Fundraising
- Meetings of the advisory group: frequency
- Annual report
- Committees

- Term of office, vacancies, and officers

- Voting, bylaws, minutes, and financial records

Considering Other Issues

Be sure to take these issues into consideration when working with your school advisory group:

1. Membership

- Recruiting, training, and retaining group members

- Achieving meaningful diversity on the group

2. Meetings

- Arranging logistics of group meetings (room, coffee, arrangement of furniture)

- Running effective meetings

- Scheduling regular meetings with the chair (e.g., once a month)

- Working with the chair to prepare the agenda a week in advance of meetings

3. Process

- Developing strategies for setting goals and building consensus in the group

- Inviting members of the group to sit on most, if not all, school committees

- Giving personal invitations for school events to the chair and the community representative

- Planning staff presentations to the group regarding curriculum, student assessment, etc.

- Finding a focus for the group

Finding a Focus

Clear goals bring people together and give them a purpose for collaborating. Your school advisory group may have too many priorities, unclear priorities, or no priorities. The result may be little momentum, wasted resources, and diminished support.

TIPS　Possible goals for the school advisory group might be

- to improve literacy,

- to improve student behavior,

- to promote parental involvement,

- to improve the physical appearance of the school,

- to focus on healthy lifestyles.

Leading the school advisory group through a planning process can be very rewarding.

Soliciting Views of the School Advisory Group

Principals are required to solicit the views of the school advisory group regarding

- local code of conduct,

- school policies or guidelines regarding appropriate dress of pupils,

- school action plans for improvement based on data.

> The major focus of school councils is to support and enhance learning for all students by developing powerful partnerships between schools, families and communities.
>
> —M. Fullan, Dean,
> Ontario Institute for Studies in Education/University of Toronto

SCHOOL ADVISORY GROUPS AND THE ROLE OF THE PRINCIPAL

Roles and Responsibilities of School Advisory Group Members: The Principal

The school principal must be a member of the school advisory group, as he or she is an important link between the group and the school. (In fact, a meeting cannot be considered a meeting of the school advisory group unless the principal or delegated vice-principal is in attendance.) However, the principal may or may not be a voting member of the group.

The principal

- **distributes promptly** to each member the material for distribution and posts the material in a school location accessible to parents;

- **acts as a resource** to the group on laws, regulations, and district policies;

- **attends all group meetings**, unless this responsibility has been delegated to the vice-principal;

- **considers each recommendation** made by the group and returns to the group with the action taken in response to the recommendation;

- **solicits views on matters** pertaining to the establishment or amendment of school policies or guidelines relating to student achievement, accountability of the education system to parents, and the communication of plans to the public;

- **may participate** on any committees established by the group;

- **may solicit the views** of the group on any matter;

- **observes** the group's code of ethics and established bylaws.

The School Advisory Group's Role in the Selection and Placement of Principals

School districts may consult with school advisory groups on the process and criteria applicable to the selection and placement of principals and vice-principals. However, school advisory groups will not have a direct role in selecting principals and vice-principals for their respective schools.

EFFECTIVE SCHOOL ADVISORY GROUPS

 Characteristics of Effective School Advisory Groups

Effective school advisory groups

- focus on student learning and the best interests of all students,

- are actively involved in setting school priorities for improving student achievement,

- promote meaningful parental and community involvement and actively seek the views of their school communities,

- have a clear understanding of their roles and responsibilities,

- include members who represent the diverse views of their school communities,

- keep well informed about school and district policies and procedures,

- have clear and consistent processes for decision making,

- communicate with the community about their activities,

- maintain high ethical standards,

- have members who have developed mutual trust and respect for one another.

> In many areas, particularly in urban centers where there are greater numbers of immigrants, it is especially important to find ways of encouraging participation from the various and diverse ethno-cultural groups that make up the school community.

What If Disputes Arise Between Members of the School Advisory Group?

School advisory groups may establish a bylaw that, in accordance with any applicable policies established by the district, establishes a conflict resolution process for internal disputes. A conflict resolution process may have the principal perform the role of mediator or arbitrator, or it may rely on other district personnel to provide an outside perspective and relative impartiality in this regard.

For further information, see Chapter 7, "Managing Conflict and Difficult People."

School Advisory Groups and Confidentiality

School advisory groups are not entitled to receive confidential student information, nor is it appropriate for them to attempt to consult with principals or school district personnel about decisions relating to specific individual students. Principals should ensure that discussions about staffing remain general, without any focus on individual teachers. Teachers are entitled to attend all meetings of the group, just as any member of the public is entitled to do.

Although this action is not specifically legislated, the principal ought to review the school advisory group's annual written report to ensure that the group has not included any confidential student information in the report. If the group has included potentially defamatory statements about school staff or other individuals, and the principal is concerned about the school district's liability, the principal may wish to consult with the district staff about editing the report before it is posted or distributed.

Get to Know the Community

If you're invited, attend the school advisory group meeting in June, prior to starting your new position in September.

Listen actively to learn as much as you can about your school community from students, parents, staff, superintendent, trustees—anyone who knows the lay of the land.

Attend functions at your new school to meet staff, students, and the community.

The Voice of Experience

13 School Organization and Scheduling

At a Glance

- Getting Started
  Key Questions
  Goals
  Information Gathering
  A Checklist
- An Overview
  Process
  Timelines
- Implementation Challenges
  Constant Change
  Class Size and School Size Considerations
  *Strategies for a Range of Courses in Small or Isolated
    Schools*
- Models for School Organization and Scheduling
  Scheduling
  Balanced School Day
  Class and Student Groupings
  Grade Configurations
  Program Configurations
  E-learning, Virtual Schools, and Distance Education
  *Implementing a New School Organization or Scheduling
    Model*

→ **GETTING STARTED**

Key Questions

Before making *any* changes, ensure that you have gathered all relevant data. Any changes you make may be received with hostility, so proceed with caution.

When it's time for you and your administrative team to start working on next year's school organization and schedule, consider the following key questions.

1. What are the contractual obligations set out in the collective agreement?

2. What is your staffing allocation?

3. What flexibility do you have in the utilization of your staffing allocation?

4. How should the staffing committee, the union, the whole staff, and the school advisory group be involved in school organization and scheduling?

5. What are the goals for the school's schedule?

6. What information and tools do you need to develop the schedule?

7. What are the steps in creating the school's master schedule?

8. What are the challenges in implementing the schedule?

9. What models and approaches are currently being used?

10. How do class size and the school size affect scheduling?

Goals

Your goals for school organization and scheduling may include some of the following:

- Increasing instructional time for students and reducing transition time

- Providing common planning time for teachers and staff development opportunities

- Offering programs by specialist teachers (e.g., physical and health education, music)

- Implementing online courses and distance education

Remember, your organizational and scheduling objectives must meet all mandated requirements; for example:

- Collective agreement provisions

- District policies and procedures

- District class size and teaching load stipulations

Information Gathering

You or your designate will begin gathering information when it is released by the district in order to start building the master schedule and create the overall school organization for the following school year. Much of this initial information will change before school begins in September; it is important to monitor these changes regularly. Information from district staff in planning, transportation, and human resources will impact school organization. Do not hesitate to ask for their assistance.

✔️ A Checklist

When you start planning your school organization and schedule, consider the following factors:

1. Collective agreements

   District policies and procedures

   Staffing and class size requirements mandated by the school district and collective agreements

   Planning time and teaching time mandated by the school district and collective agreements

2. Facilities and equipment constraints

   District transportation procedures and shared busing arrangements

3. Projected student enrollment

   Kindergarten registration or option sheets for new and returning secondary students

   Criteria for acceptance into specialized programs not offered in a student's home school

   Attendance procedures

4. Number of staff positions (teaching and nonteaching) that the enrollment generates

   Positions allocated for vice-principals and department heads

Positions allocated for classroom teachers, resource teachers, and specialist teachers

5. Delivery model for special education services and programs and for English as a second language (ESL) programs

   Itinerant teachers or other staff who are shared between two or more schools

   Teacher qualifications and individual teaching preferences and strengths

   Teaching and learning issues (e.g., uninterrupted mornings for primary grades, cooperative education placements for secondary students, common planning time for teaching teams)

6. Software available to generate timetables and supervision schedules

   Expertise on staff regarding school scheduling and available training opportunities

⊙ AN OVERVIEW

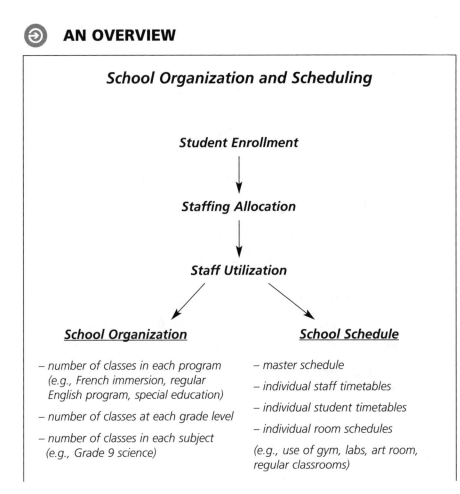

School Organization and Scheduling

Student Enrollment

↓

Staffing Allocation

↓

Staff Utilization

↙ ↘

School Organization

– *number of classes in each program (e.g., French immersion, regular English program, special education)*

– *number of classes at each grade level*

– *number of classes in each subject (e.g., Grade 9 science)*

School Schedule

– *master schedule*

– *individual staff timetables*

– *individual student timetables*

– *individual room schedules*

(e.g., use of gym, labs, art room, regular classrooms)

– number of students in each class

– delivery model for special programs

– assignment of teachers to subjects and classes

Note:
1. The school schedule is just one of the elements of school organization.
2. The school schedule involves the use of time, staff, and space to promote student achievement.

The physical plant (e.g., stairs, portables, specialty rooms, gym space, rooms for withdrawal programs) impacts both the school organization and the school schedule.

 Process

1. Follow the district's staffing process, timelines, and procedures from start to finish.

2. Scheduling is a complex process involving collaborative decision-making.

3. Follow provisions in collective agreements regarding staffing committees, staff consultation, etc.

4. Educate the school advisory group and staff about the scheduling process.

5. Maintain accurate, up-to-date records on enrollment statistics, number of classes, students' subject choices, staffing allocation, etc.

6. Review ongoing changes in the school organization and schedule with all stakeholders.

7. Help staff, parents, and students to focus on student learning needs and how students can be best served by the school's organization.

8. Once the master schedule is developed, it becomes the basis for all other schedules, including withdrawal programs, student assembly schedules, and other special events.

9. The school's schedule, organization, and teaching assignments can have a major impact on school climate and staff morale.

Timelines

Timelines will vary by district.

January/February

1. Prepare a timeline for the completion of scheduling tasks and assign responsibility centers.

2. Follow collective agreement provisions to involve staff through staffing and school organization committees.

3. Discuss with staff members their teaching qualifications and preferences for the coming year.

4. Revise or develop forms for option sheets, requests to drop a course, etc.

5. Revise or develop a program to assist students with the transition between grades or schools.

6. Prepare a preliminary report of student choices and the number of students for each grade level.

7. Schedule a visit to feeder schools to brief incoming students and their teachers. Brief returning students about next year's program and schedule.

8. Schedule parent information evening(s).

9. Schedule kindergarten registration and Grade 9 registration; collect secondary school option sheets.

10. Discuss with your supervisor any impact on the existing physical plant to accommodate changes in enrollment and program for September.

March/April

1. Determine the number of minutes for breaks, recesses, class changes, and lunch in keeping with the collective agreements and districtwide policies.

2. Assign the number of classes to each grade level.

3. Assign the number of sections to each department.

4. Cancel courses and programs for which there is insufficient enrollment.

5. Combine classes or grade levels to make viable groupings.

6. Match classes and courses to specific rooms and instructional areas.

7. Prepare a master timetable.

8. Review schedule and revise scheduling conflicts.

9. In a school newsletter, publish the school's policy regarding requests for changes from students and parents.

10. Schedule meetings for teachers who have a change in schedule within the school. If the revision requires the teacher to teach between two schools, check the collective agreements for any provisions regarding the schedule. All revisions should be done in consultation with the supervisor.

May/June

1. Follow collective agreement stipulations and district timelines regarding staffing.

2. Revise students' course selections to reflect any cancelled classes.

3. Update staff lists.

4. Conduct interviews for vacant staff positions if staffing is not done centrally.

5. Evaluate effectiveness of current year's schedule in supporting student needs and achievement.

IMPLEMENTATION CHALLENGES

Constant Change

Regardless of the degree of planning and monitoring, be prepared to deal with a number of challenges and unexpected events when managing the school organization and scheduling. Develop strategies to address

- parent requests for specific teachers or change of teachers or courses,

- cancelled courses and programs,

- unanticipated increases or decreases in enrollment in September,

- difficulty in providing supervision and on-call coverage given the constraints of collective agreement requirements,

- new school additions or renovations that might not be completed for September.

Class Size and School Size Considerations

While the district stipulates average class sizes for both elementary and secondary schools, you will want to be aware of the research on class size and school size. Review the research on class size, school size, multi-age groupings, etc., if this is a priority. Understand the difference between average class size and the overall pupil-teacher ratio in the school when creating the school's master schedule. Class size does not refer to pupil-teacher ratio.

Educate the staff, parents, and school advisory group about the effects of school size and class size on school organization.

Monitor class size to ensure it complies with district requirements.

If you have concerns, monitor and document the impact of school size on student achievement, support for students with special needs, school climate, staff productivity and burnout, student behavior and discipline, etc. Share these concerns with your superintendent of schools.

Strategies for a Range of Courses in Small or Isolated Schools

TIPS   Possible strategies to alleviate the problems of providing a range of courses in small or isolated schools could include

- Providing opportunities for staff to acquire additional qualifications in different areas

- Offering different types of courses and courses at different grades within the same class

- Supplementing the school program with correspondence courses or with courses taken through private study

- Offering courses through distance education and other forms of electronic course delivery, including closed-circuit television

- Offering courses through the cooperative education mode of delivery to enable students to gain more credits for those courses

MODELS FOR SCHOOL ORGANIZATION AND SCHEDULING

You will want to review a number of options before making any significant changes in the school's organization and schedule. Several ideas for further research are listed below.

Scheduling

Block scheduling

- Parallel (class divided into two groups, one group staying with the classroom teacher and the other attending specialist classes)

- Intensive (two core classes coupled with three-year-long electives)

- Four-block day (four 85- to 100-minute classes per semester)

- Alternating A/B plan (eight blocks of classes over two days)

Extended day (late starts/early evenings)

Flexible scheduling/independent study

Four-day school week/extended day

Full day/alternate day kindergarten

Shifts

Students attending classes in more than one school per week

Traditional six- or seven-period day with partial or full rotary

Two- to seven-day cycles

Two, three, or four semesters per year

> The schedule a school follows is a very important component of student learning, and with so many scheduling options available, it is easy to become lost in a maze of research and recommendations without arriving at any real conclusion. . . .
>
> What works well in one school may not work at all in another.
>
> —J. Fager, *Scheduling Alternatives: Options for Success* (www.nwrel.org)

Balanced School Day

The *Balanced School Day* schedule divides the school day into three 100-minute blocks of instructional time with two nutrition breaks instead of the traditional recesses and lunch hour. This schedule creates equally balanced teaching/learning blocks of time as illustrated in the table below.

Sample Schedule

Time	Activity
8:50 A.M.	Entry
8:55 A.M.–9:45 A.M.	Period 1
9:45 A.M.–10:35 A.M.	Period 2
10:35 A.M.–11:20 A.M.	Nutrition Break #1
11:20 A.M.–12:10 P.M.	Period 3
12:10 P.M.–1:00 P.M.	Period 4
1:00 P.M.–1:45 P.M.	Nutrition Break #2
1:45 P.M.–2:35 P.M.	Period 5
2:35 P.M.–3:25 P.M.	Period 6
3:25 P.M.	Dismissal

The day is framed around two 45-minute nutrition breaks. These breaks are divided between a time for healthy eating and a time for outside fresh air, socialization, and exercise (20 minutes for eating and 20 minutes for play with 5 minutes for entry and transition). This schedule then provides for 100-minute blocks of time for teaching and learning.

Class and Student Groupings

Homerooms

House plan or theme-based academies

Looping

Multi-age classrooms with combined courses

Pull-out and withdrawal programs

Single sex classes and schools

Grade Configurations

7–12

9–12

PreK/K–12

PreK/K–6

PreK/K–8

Middle schools and junior high schools

Program Configurations

Magnet schools

Alternative elementary and secondary programs

Charter schools

Twinned schools: two or more small schools at different locations that share a principal

Schools-within-schools: one or more small schools within a larger host school

Multiplex: one building specifically intended to house several small schools

E-learning, Virtual Schools, and Distance Education

Distance education courses are credit courses that are offered by schools through various technological means, such as teleconferencing, the Internet, and videoconferencing. In geographically large school districts or in districts which require small schools where all programs cannot be offered in every school, some boards offer specific courses through these electronic means. This is also an alternative delivery method for some special needs students. These programs are monitored by qualified teachers and accredited by the district.

Implementing a New School Organization or Scheduling Model

1. Involve your supervisor early in the process; changing the schedule may require district approval, building renovations, transportation changes, or staffing modifications.

2. Ensure sufficient time is allocated to gather information, consult all stakeholders, and design and, if possible, field-test the model.

3. Create a research or steering committee of staff, students, and parents.

4. Survey staff, students, and parents about their perspectives on the school's schedule and how it affects their family and work responsibilities, as well as student achievement.

5. Make certain the staff members understand the changes in instructional strategies required with a particular organizational model.

6. Ensure staff have access to staff development activities that support implementation.

7. Keep the school advisory group, staff, parents, students, and teachers' union informed in order to promote understanding and reduce conflict.

8. Keep in mind prerequisite courses, course sequencing, number of instructional minutes in the day, and minutes per course or subject. In secondary schools, most students must be able to graduate within a required time.

9. Design a procedure that will accommodate students transferring from a school with a different schedule or organizational structure.

10. Monitor the impact of any scheduling changes and share evaluation of the data with all stakeholders.

Manage Change Carefully

Don't change the school's organization or procedures right away. There are likely very good reasons for the way things are done. Go slowly with change.

Everything does not have to be done immediately.

The Voice of Experience

PART II

Teaching and Learning

School Programs

At a Glance

- Getting Started
    - *Building a Learning Community*
    - *Reviewing School Programs*
    - *Pulling It All Together*
- Curriculum Implementation
    - *The Principal's Role*
    - *Curriculum Implementation Timelines*
    - *Assessment and Evaluation of Programs:*
        - *Data Driven Improvement*
    - *Assessing the Implementation of the Curriculum*
- Student Assessment, Evaluation, and Reporting
    - *Assessment and Evaluation of Student Achievement:*
        - *An Overview*
    - *Reporting Student Achievement*

→ GETTING STARTED

Building a Learning Community

1. What is a learning community?

Building a learning community in your school building is the focus of creating an environment centered around students. A professional learning community is about learners having a passion for learning, not about bricks and walls and resources. It is about individuals who share a common vision of the learning environment they want to create. It is about individuals who pursue the best for themselves and for others who live in this community of thought. Together they explore, discover, and share in the design of a road map for their journey of learning. Creative ideas and solutions are fostered. Collective thinking and action is required. Progress is expected and measured. Challenges and obstacles provide more opportunities to learn. It is all about passion, commitment, and believing that you can create your own vision of an effective school.

A professional learning community is built upon the resilient foundations of

- **Mission**—Why do we exist?
- **Vision**—What do we hope to become?
- **Values**—How must we behave?
- **Goals**—What steps and when?

Building a professional learning community requires schools to examine and respond to the key questions surrounding the four foundations. As curriculum leaders, principals must begin their journey with an understanding and commitment to this process. Patience and persistence will keep you on the course.

2. How to build one in your school

Step one is to form learning teams. These are small groups of professionals who agree to experiment with new ideas and meet regularly for a specific period to time to share experiences guided by specific goals and purposes. The foundations for effective learning teams are collaboration, effective inquiry, action orientation, and experimentation. The effort to transform a school into a professional learning community is more likely to be sustained when teachers

- participate in reflective dialogue,
- observe and react to one another's teaching,
- jointly develop curriculum and assessment practices,
- work together to implement new programs and strategies,
- share lesson plans and material,
- collectively engage in problem-solving, action research, and continuous improvement practices.

The principal's role is to facilitate the work of learning by creating time for teachers to collaborate. This can be done by examining the school schedule and finding ways to free up time for meetings.

On a cyclical basis, the learning community, led by the principal, must review and assess achievement of goals; reflect on results; refocus on mission, vision, and values; and revise the school improvement plan accordingly.

Further Reading and Study

DuFour, R., and Eaker, R. (1998) *Professional Learning Communities at Work: Best Practices for Enhancing Student Achievement*

DuFour, R., Eaker, R., and Burnette, R. (2002) *Getting Started: Reculturing Schools to Become Professional Learning Communities*

Reviewing School Programs

1. Review your district's policies and procedures related to school programs, curriculum, and student achievement.

2. Review instructional programs.
   - Which instructional programs are offered at your school?
   - How many students are enrolled in each program?
   - Invite key staff members to brief you on each of the instructional programs.

3. Ask the principal (or appropriate staff member) to brief you regarding the following:
   - The instructional activities currently offered at the school
   - The history of activities at the school

4. Obtain copies of all relevant curriculum documents.

5. Review the course outlines and long-range plans for all courses offered at the school.

6. As you read student report cards and review them with teachers, you will learn a lot about school programs, individual student success, overall levels of student achievement, and the quality of student assessment, evaluation, and reporting at the school.

7. Be visible in the school; observe instructional programs in action.

> Effective principals demand content and instruction that ensure student achievement of agreed-upon academic standards. These principals:
>
> - hire and retain high quality teachers and hold them responsible for student learning
>
> - monitor alignment of curriculum with standards, school goals and assessments
>
> - observe classroom practices to ensure that all students are meaningfully engaged in active learning
>
> - provide up-to-date technology and instructional materials
>
> - review and analyze student work to determine whether students are being taught to standard
>
> *—Leading Learning Communities: Standards for What Principals Should Know and Be Able to Do,* National Association of Elementary School Principals

Pulling It All Together

As an instructional leader, you will pull together your knowledge and skills from a number of key areas in order to support school programs and student learning. These include your knowledge and skills in the following key areas:

Program

- Current research

- District policies and procedures

- Curriculum and expectations

- Scheduling and school organizational structures

- Creative use of school facilities

Teachers

- Teaching and learning styles; brain compatible teaching and learning

- Staffing (selection and assignment)

- Teacher supervision and evaluation

- Staff development

Students

- Characteristics of students at different stages of development

Policy

- Inclusion, cultural equity, and antidiscrimination and antiviolence education

- Student assessment, evaluation, and reporting practices and procedures

- Assessment, evaluation, and the utilization of data

- Budgeting that supports learning priorities

- School profile and goals based on standardized testing results

> These areas are all interrelated. Whether you are hiring a new teacher or working with the staff budget committee, you are making decisions in support of student learning.

TIPS

> Effective principals serve as instructional leaders in four ways:
>
> They possess a substantial knowledge base and they plan, implement and evaluate instructional programs collaboratively.
>
> —*Principals for Our Changing Schools:*
> *The Knowledge and Skill Base,*
> S. D. Thompson, p. 8-3

CURRICULUM IMPLEMENTATION

The Principal's Role

As the principal, you will lead the curriculum implementation process at the school.

The school leader's role is to

- set the vision and mission (in consultation with all stakeholders);

- provide staff development;

- motivate, coach, and set expectations;

- provide resources and time;
- identify vehicles to motivate curriculum discussion;
- model desired behaviors and attitudes.

⊙ Curriculum Implementation Timelines

In concert with districtwide directions, support a curriculum implementation timeline over a three- to five-year cycle. Remember, implementation is a process, not an event. Share this timeline with all stakeholders. Determine timelines for each stage of implementation:

- Familiarization
- Initial introduction
- Partial implementation
- Continuing implementation
- Full implementation

Determine timelines for each stage of curriculum review:

- Initial reactions
- Ongoing, formative review
- Formal, summative review

> The best way for a principal to approach situations of impossible overload is to take the stance that "we are going to implement a few things especially well, and implement other priorities as well as we would have anyway."
>
> —*What's Worth Fighting For in the Principalship?*
> M. Fullan, p. 28

Assessment and Evaluation of Programs: Data Driven Improvement

Teachers and principals should systematically review

- course content,
- instructional strategies, and
- assessment procedures

and make the program changes needed to improve their students' achievements.

The analysis of the results of

- districtwide assessments,

- statewide assessments, and

- national and international testing

provides additional information on student achievement and program effectiveness, complementing the program assessments conducted by teachers and principals.

Where areas for improvement are identified through such analysis, schools and districts should work with parents and other representatives from the community to address these areas in their school and district action plans.

Assessing the Implementation of the Curriculum

The district will likely have a required process for assessing curriculum implementation. You and your staff may wish to design rubrics using performance levels and expectations.

Just Beginning	Approaching Implementation	Implementing	Extensively Implementing
I use some . . .	I use many . . .	I regularly use . . .	I effectively use . . .

Expectations you may wish to assess include, among others:

- Planning, organizing, and delivering programs based on the overall and specific expectations

- Designing performance tasks to assess multiple expectations across the achievement categories

- Planning program activities that include expectations from various subjects

- Using a range of instructional strategies and appropriate resources to deliver programs

- Ensuring that the individual learning needs of all students are met

STUDENT ASSESSMENT, EVALUATION, AND REPORTING

As you monitor the implementation of the curriculum, you will also want to monitor student assessment and evaluation practices and the reporting of student achievement.

Assessment and Evaluation of Student Achievement: An Overview

The primary purpose of assessment and evaluation is to improve student learning. Assessment and evaluation are based on the curriculum expectations and the achievement levels outlined in the curriculum policy document for each discipline. In order to ensure that assessment and evaluation are valid and reliable, and that they lead to the improvement of student learning, teachers must use appropriate strategies. The items below can be used as a checklist to help you monitor the assessment and evaluation strategies being used in your school.

Teachers must use strategies that

- address both what students learn and how well they learn;

- are based both on the categories of knowledge and skills and on the achievement level descriptions given in the achievement chart that appears in the curriculum policy document for each discipline;

- are varied in nature, administered over a period of time, and designed to provide opportunities for students to demonstrate the full range of their learning;

- are appropriate for the learning activities used, the purposes of instruction, and the needs and experiences of the students;

- are fair to all students;

- accommodate the needs of exceptional students, consistent with the strategies outlined in their individual education plans;

- accommodate the needs of students who are learning the language of instruction;

- ensure that each student is given clear directions for improvement;

- promote students' ability to assess their own learning and to set specific goals;

- include the use of samples of students' work that provide evidence of their achievement;

- are communicated clearly to students and parents at the beginning of the course and at other appropriate points throughout the course.

Reporting Student Achievement

The Report Card

Follow your district's guidelines regarding reporting student achievement. Student achievement must be communicated formally to students and parents by means of a reporting system. Provide staff with guidelines and timelines for the completion of any report cards. Provide staff new to the technology with training regarding the completion of electronic report cards.

Provide regular training for all staff to develop consistency in student assessment, evaluation, and reporting. This will involve grade level discussions regarding specific curriculum expectations, the levels of achievement, assessment rubrics, student work samples, etc. Facilitate communication among the various teachers who report on a student's achievement.

Read and sign student report cards. Share this task with the vice-principal. Follow up where necessary.

Meet with teachers individually to discuss the quality of their reporting and the achievement of individual students.

Note: You will be required to report on other aspects of student assessment and evaluation as well, for example, standardized testing programs.

TIPS

Parent-Teacher Conferences

Encourage and support teachers as they conduct parent-teacher conferences. Attend conferences if requested to do so.

Provide staff with training for conducting successful parent conferences. If your district does not have a conference guide for teachers, find or create a list of suggestions and share them at a staff meeting. Both new teachers and experienced teachers will benefit from these discussions.

Conference tips should include what to do before, during, and after a parent interview to ensure its success.

Ongoing Reporting to Parents

In addition to report cards and scheduled schoolwide parent-teacher conferences, encourage teachers to communicate with parents regularly through a variety of strategies, and support them in this process. Strategies might include informal notes, regular daily feedback in some circumstances, communication books and student agendas, phone calls, class newsletters, and e-mails. The goal is to keep parents informed and to avoid surprises.

Remember: Education Web sites are the places where many parents get their information.

As you review the programs offered at the school, observe the relationship between

- the written curriculum,

- the taught curriculum, and

- the tested curriculum.

Focus on fundamentals:

- Curriculum

- Instruction

- Assessment

- Professional culture

—What's Worth Fighting For in the Principalship?
M. Fullan, p. 28

Be Prepared

Manage time wisely to allow for the multitude of tasks that present themselves. Don't take on too many priorities at once.

Start things on time. Don't punish the punctual.

The Voice of Experience

Special Education and English as a Second Language

A Special Education Program is . . .

a program for an exceptional pupil based on, and modified by, the results of continuous assessment and evaluation, and that includes a plan containing specific objectives and an outline of educational services that meet the needs of the pupil.

➔ SPECIAL EDUCATION: GETTING STARTED

1. **Review**

    a. District policies and procedures regarding special education. These might cover a variety of topics such as

- special education programs and services,
- academic intervention education programs,
- psychological assessments.

b. The district special education handbook.

c. Special education parent brochures prepared by the district. Remember, if the district has a *Parent's Guide to Special Education,* you must provide a copy to the parents of a student going through the referral process for the first time.

d. The special education forms created by your district. These might include everything from forms to be used for obtaining parental consent for psychology testing, to a principal's checklist for tracking all the documentation leading up to a placement.

Determine your district's process for central programs and placement and school-based programs and placement.

Gather together all legislation relating to special education.

Regulations set out the legal responsibilities regarding special education.

They also provide comprehensive procedures for

- the identification of exceptional students;

- the placement of those students in educational settings where the special education programs and services appropriate to their needs can be delivered;

- review of the identification of exceptional students and their placement.

2. School-Based Staff

Meet with all special education teachers and other relevant staff for an overview of special education programs and services in the school. Meet with all concerned staff at the school for an initial briefing. Clarify your own roles and the responsibilities of concerned staff. Arrange to meet regularly with all concerned staff for updates.

Follow the tracking system for all required documentation and activities, such as consent forms, referral forms, student assessments and staff/parent debriefings afterward, initial referrals, individual education plans (IEPs), and reviews.

Look for links between special education staff and programs and other general education services and programs; for example, the regular program, English as a second or other language programs, and guidance services.

3. Relationships

Manage the expectations of staff and parents of exceptional students. Build positive relationships with students, parents, and staff involved in special education.

4. Itinerant Staff

Consult with the special education professional resource team and individuals assigned to your school; for example, teacher diagnostician, psychometrician, psychiatrist, social worker, psychologist, speech-language pathologist, audiologist, occupational therapist, or physiotherapist. Clarify your own special education roles and responsibilities and those of members of the special needs team that serves your school.

Review where the itinerant professionals work while at the school. Ensure that they have appropriate space to meet with students, parents, and staff. Balance privacy with student protection.

Ensure that itinerant staff understand their reporting responsibilities.

Inform itinerant professionals about events at the school; send them the school newsletter, invite them to staff meetings and staff get-togethers, assign mailboxes, include them on electronic staff conferences, and invite them to make presentations to staff and parents.

Obtain and record contact numbers of key team members (e.g., social workers) for use in an emergency during the day or after school hours.

5. District-Based Staff

Contact the coordinator or director of special education at the district office.

Create a list of local community support services: agencies, advocates, and associations related to various aspects of special education and exceptional students.

6. Exceptional Students

Find out if any referrals are pending from before your arrival.

Review the student records and individual education plans (IEPs) of all identified students.

Review the list of all classified students in school and those with academic intervention support.

Determine the percentage of these exceptional students identified in each category; for example, learning disabled, intellectually gifted.

Determine what percentage of the student population has been identified as exceptional.

7. Monitoring

Get to know exceptional students as individuals.

Attend case conferences for individual students as appropriate.

Track the progress of exceptional students.

Monitor the delivery of in-class program modifications as outlined in students' IEPs.

8. Professional Development

Provide for in-service to meet identified needs of special education staff.

Arrange for teachers and assistants to visit special education programs in other schools.

Visit other schools yourself to observe classes and talk with principals about special education issues.

ROLES AND RESPONSIBILITIES OF THE PRINCIPAL

Communication Requirements

Principals must communicate

- school district expectations to staff;
- district policies and procedures about special education to staff, students, and parents;
- with parents and with district staff to determine the most appropriate program for exceptional students;
- with parents in the development of their child's IEP, and provide them with a copy of the IEP.

 Duties

Principals must do the following:

- Through district policies and procedures, carry out duties as outlined in regulations and in policy and program memoranda

- Assign qualified staff to teach special education classes
- Conduct the identification and placement of exceptional students, through referral according to the procedures in school board policies and regulations
- Supervise the development, implementation, and review of a student's IEP, including a transition plan, according to the needs of the student
- Supervise the delivery of the program as set out in the IEP
- Request appropriate assessments and parental consent
- Know budgetary implications of special education programs

Categories of Exceptionality
Recognized by the Education Act

Behavior   Communication   Intellectual

Physical   Multiple

REFERRAL ROUTINES

Referral routines will vary from district to district. Remember to follow your district's procedure regarding Identification, Placement, and Review Committees.

Utilize Timeline

Meeting Requested

(Within 15–30 days of request)

Parent receives

- acknowledgement of request,
- Parents' guide,
- notification of referral meeting,
- details of the meeting (date, time, place).

(Before the meeting and as soon as possible after receipt of information)

Identification, Placement, and Review Committee chair sends parent (and student if 16 or older)

- information about student received by Identification, Placement, and Review Committee.

Identification, Placement, and Review Committee Meeting

- Student's strengths and needs documented
- Permission for further assessment and diagnosis documented
- Categories and definitions of exceptionalities identified
- Recommendations made about program and services
- As soon as possible after decision, statement of decision agreed to by relevant parties

After Decision

Parent may

- agree and sign consent form,
- make no response,
- request further discussion, or
- disagree and file appeal with special education appeal board.

If parent agrees or makes no response,

- school completes IEP; parents get a copy.

If parent wishes further discussion,

- request for second meeting;
- as soon as possible after the second meeting, notice of results sent to relevant persons, along with reasons for changes if there is a revised decision.

If parent disagrees

- parent files notice of appeal with appropriate district supervisor.

After Second Identification, Placement, and Review Committee Meeting

Parent may

- sign consent form or
- make no response (district then implements placement and develops IEP).

If parent disagrees,

- parent files notice of appeal with appropriate district supervisor.

A Range of Special Education Placements

School districts are to provide as full a range of placements as possible to meet the needs of exceptional students. These might include the following:

- Regular classroom placement with monitoring
- Regular classroom placement with consulting support to the classroom teacher and/or direct support to the student
- Regular classroom placement with withdrawal support for one-on-one or small group assistance
- Part-time regular classroom placement and part-time special education classroom
- Full-time special education classroom
- A special day school
- Full-time placement in an alternate setting

ESL AND ESOL: GETTING STARTED

1. **Review District's**

   a. Policies and procedures regarding English as a Second Language (ESL) and English for Speakers of Other Languages (ESOL)

   b. Handbook

   c. Forms

   d. Parent brochures

   e. Process for assessment and placement of incoming ESL/ESOL students

2. **District Services**

   Meet the district ESL coordinator. If there is a central ESL welcome center for your district, visit it and introduce yourself to the staff. Identify district resources for translators, interpreters, and settlement agencies.

3. **School Services**

   Review your school office routines for registration and documentation of new students. Meet with the school ESL/ESOL teacher or coordinator regularly:

a. Clarify your relative roles and responsibilities.

b. Agree on a tracking system for documentation, including registration, assessment, and placement. Involve your office coordinator in this discussion.

Meet with all ESL/ESOL teachers and educational assistants for an overview of the programs and services in the school. Look for links between ESL/ESOL staff and programs and other school staff and programs; for example, the regular program, special education program, and guidance services.

4. Relationships

Build positive relationships with all ESL/ESOL students, parents, and staff. Manage the expectations of staff and parents of ESL/ESOL students. Enlist the support of district resources to ensure that all procedures are culturally appropriate.

5. Itinerant Staff

Consult with any itinerant ESL/ESOL teachers, liaison officers, or translators assigned to your school:

a. Clarify relative roles and responsibilities.

b. Review where itinerant staff work while at the school. Ensure that they have appropriate space to meet with students, parents, and staff. Balance privacy with student protection.

c. Inform itinerant staff about events at the school; send them the school newsletter, invite them to staff meetings and staff get-togethers, assign mailboxes, include them on electronic staff conferences, and invite them to make presentations to staff and parents.

d. Ensure that itinerant staff understand their reporting duties.

Create a list of local community support services: agencies, advocates, and associations related to various issues concerning new and various cultural communities.

6. ESL/ESOL Students

a. Review the student records of all ESL/ESOL students.

b. Determine how many students speak each of the first languages represented at the school.

   c. Review the list of all ESL/ESOL students in school.

   d. Determine what percentage of the student population speaks English as a second language.

7. Monitoring

Get to know ESL/ESOL students as individuals. Attend case conferences and parent interviews for individual students as appropriate. Track the progress of ESL/ESOL students. Monitor the delivery of in-class program modifications for ESOL students.

8. Professional Development

Provide professional development activities to meet identified needs of ESL/ESOL staff. Arrange for staff to visit the district's ESL Reception Center and ESL programs in other schools. Provide all staff members (teaching and nonteaching) with professional learning opportunities focusing on equity, diversity, and inclusion. Invite members of various ethnic communities to brief you and the staff on relevant issues.

Visit other schools yourself to observe classes and talk with principals about ESL/ESOL issues.

9. Outreach

Look for ways to welcome parents who do not speak English. Host special parent nights using simultaneous interpretation. Translate key school communications into the main languages spoken by parents. Find out if the district can help with these translations. Reflect cultural diversity of the school in both the instructional and coinstructional program.

Monitor and implement district policy on inclusion throughout the school.

Be Visible

Start the day with two walk-throughs—the first as staff are arriving, the second after the students have arrived.

Make time for students every single day.

The Voice of Experience

16

Data Driven School Improvement

➔ GETTING STARTED

> The overall objective of school improvement planning is to enhance student achievement.

1. Follow your district policies and procedures regarding data driven school improvement.

    Follow the steps outlined in your district's handbook regarding analyzing and reporting testing results and designing a school profile and action plan.

2. Examine all student assessment data, which will include the following items:

    Individual student assessments by teachers

    School report card statistics

Schoolwide assessments at various grade levels

Districtwide assessment programs

National and international testing programs:

- Third International Mathematics and Science Study (TIMSS)
- School Achievement Indicators Program (SAIP)
- Progress in International Reading Literacy Study (PIRLS)
- Program for International Student Achievement (PISA)

3. Review the school's

- data,
- profile,
- improvement plans and results.

4. Consult with the school improvement committee regarding progress to date.

5. Review resources regarding school improvement planning.

EFFECTIVE SCHOOL IMPROVEMENT PLANNING

Developing a School Improvement Plan

Example:

A Sample School Improvement Plan

Goal: 1. To increase positive student behavior

Performance Target: A. By the end of year three, there will be a 50 percent reduction in the number of reported bullying incidents.

B. By the end of year three, there will be a 40 percent reduction in the number of behavior infractions.

Focus	Strategies	Indicators of Success	Time Lines	Responsibility	Status Update	Revisions
A. Bullying						

Other goals that might form part of this school improvement plan are

2. To help parents support their children's learning at home
3. To raise the overall level of students' writing skills as measured in standard assessments

---

In planning improvement, schools should establish one priority in each of these three areas:

- Curriculum delivery

- School environment

- Parental involvement

The Role of the Principal in Improvement Planning: A Checklist

The principal's roles in school improvement planning fall into three main categories:

1. Communication

2. Professional development

3. Leadership

1. Communication

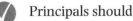 Principals should

- clearly explain the school improvement process to staff, school advisory groups, parents, and other community members;

- help staff, school advisory groups, parents, and other community members understand their role in the process and invite them to participate;

- provide the community with a school profile detailing the nature and characteristics of the school;

- ensure that everyone involved in the process receives regular communications about the improvement plan and the school's progress.

2. Professional Development

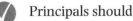 Principals should

- encourage staff to lead the development and implementation of the plan and

- provide professional development and training to staff, school advisory group members, parents, and other community members focused on the goals and strategies in the school improvement plan.

3. Leadership

 Principals should

- regularly collect data on student achievement,

- use these data in discussions with teachers regarding adjusting and improving teaching strategies,

- ensure that the school budget supports the plan's goals with those developing the school improvement plan,

- regularly assess implementation of the school improvement plan,

- communicate data as part of the plan's monitoring and evaluation process,

- lead the school and its community in celebrating successes achieved in the pursuit of the school's improvement goals.

**Further Reading Regarding
Data Driven School Improvement**

Holcomb, E. L. (1999) *Getting Excited About Data: How to Combine People, Passion, and Proof*

Manage Change Carefully

Don't push too hard when things are not going the way you want; try to remember that others will not always share your passion for a particular idea.

Change is a process, not an event.

The Voice of Experience

Staff Supervision and Performance Appraisal

17

➔ GETTING STARTED

1. Definitions and Documents

Performance appraisal refers to the evaluation of a teacher's practice.

Supervision refers to monitoring behavior and, where necessary, imposing discipline for unsatisfactory behavior.

Follow your district policies and procedures regarding the supervision (discipline) and performance appraisal of staff in all employee groups. These procedures might include the following topics:

- Supervision of employees

- Alleged employee misconduct toward a student

- Alleged harassment of an employee

- Human rights

- Progressive discipline of employees

Follow the steps outlined in your district's procedure regarding staff supervision and performance appraisal. Review all district forms related to staff supervision and performance appraisal.

2. Collective Agreements

Determine the requirements set out in relevant collective agreements for each employee group before commencing a staff discipline or performance appraisal process. (For example, a collective agreement might specify a number of days' prior notice a teacher must have in advance of a classroom visit.)

3. Past School Practice

Discuss with the vice-principal:

- Current issues and practices at the school
- Expectations concerning the respective responsibilities
- Staff supervision and performance appraisal schedule
- Past performance appraisals of individual staff members

4. Prepare Teachers

Ensure that all staff members have a copy of district performance appraisal procedures.

Host a session for staff members who wish to discuss the procedures.

Keep yourself up-to-date regarding standards for teacher performance appraisal.

When conducting teacher performance appraisals, be sure to follow your district's policies and procedures.

5. Prepare Yourself

Review your district's expectations for your role in the supervision and performance appraisal of

- Administrative staff
- Technicians; for example, the library technician, the computer technician
- Custodial staff

- Educational assistants

- Itinerant staff at the school, for example, district social workers and psychologists

- Cafeteria workers, bus drivers, multicultural officers

Know the requirements of collective agreements of unionized workers.

Identify aspects of teacher performance appraisal that you wish to explore further; for example, conferencing, classroom observation, and writing performance reports.

⊕ SUPERVISION OF VICE-PRINCIPALS

What constitutes adequate supervision of a vice-principal?

In the absence of the principal, the vice-principal is in charge of the school and performs the duties of the principal. A principal generally supervises the vice-principal, and failure to do so adequately may constitute professional misconduct. Where a principal delegates any supervisory responsibilities to a vice-principal, the following actions are recommended:

- Establish an open door policy.

- Implement a regular reporting structure on the subject matter of the delegation.

- Communicate frequently and regularly about "problem" students, staff, and other issues.

- Ensure that any reporting mechanisms put in place are utilized according to the stated intention.

- Advise all staff of the principal's ultimate responsibility for any and all problems, such that serious issues should also be reported directly to the principal regardless of any general delegation of authority.

School Guests and Volunteers Under Principal's Professional Supervision

In addition to students and staff, principals have school guests and volunteers under their supervision.

Adequate supervision of them may mean different things. The particular circumstances of each individual must be taken into account, for example, education, training, experience, and role.

STATE STANDARDS FOR TEACHER PERFORMANCE APPRAISAL

Keep yourself up-to-date on the evolving standards for teacher performance appraisal. When conducting teacher performance appraisals, be sure to follow your state's or district's policies and procedures. They will be revised to reflect any subsequent changes in regulations.

TEACHER SUPERVISION AND PERFORMANCE APPRAISAL

Terminology

1. Discipline

Always consult with your supervisor before taking disciplinary action. A sample of progressive discipline with a series of escalating consequences may look like this:

- First or minor offense: oral reprimand; verbal admonition

- Serious or repeated offense: written warning; letter of reprimand

- Major offense: suspension (with or without pay)

- Critical offense: dismissal

These consequences are not tied directly to any particular "level" of offense. Each discipline situation must be considered on its own merits. If there are repeated incidents of the same behavior, the consequences may escalate accordingly.

Disciplinary measures are dealt with in a meeting with the teacher. The teacher is advised of the right to representation in advance.

2. Written Reprimand

This letter contains

- A description of the unacceptable behavior

- A statement of expected behavior

- Consequences for noncompliance up to and including termination

3. Inappropriate or Unacceptable Behavior

Situations of inappropriate or unacceptable behavior arise when teachers violate—through their behavior—regulations, district policy, their contract or collective agreement, state or other specific standards, or other pertinent legislation.

Such situations include but are not limited to

- inappropriate language,
- inappropriate actions,
- racial or sexual harassment of colleagues or students or other human rights violations,
- chronic lateness with no satisfactory explanation,
- unauthorized absence,
- pursuing an inappropriate relationship with a student,
- criminal activity,
- other behavior generally considered professionally unacceptable.

Incidents of inappropriate or unacceptable behavior are dealt with through the discipline process.

4. Insubordination

Conduct that is threatening or contemptuous of the employer or that challenges the employer's authority is insubordinate. In the school setting, the principal represents the employer. Examples of insubordinate teacher conduct include the following:

- Refusing, without excuse or justification, to obey a direct order, when the principal has the authority to give the order
- Tearing up a written warning upon its presentation by the principal outside of a legal strike
- Picketing the school outside of a legal strike
- Composing and distributing leaflets that are critical of the principal
- Using language that is threatening or contemptuous of the principal, where such behavior involves a resistance to or defiance of the employer's authority

5. Professional Misconduct

A principal can be accused of a failure to supervise a teacher who commits professional misconduct. Examples of professional misconduct include the following:

- Providing false information or documents to any person with respect to the teacher's professional qualifications
- Inappropriately using a term, title, or designation indicating a specialization in the profession which is not specified on the teacher's certificate of qualification and registration

- Failing to maintain the standards of the profession

- Releasing or disclosing information about a student to a person other than the student or, if the student is a minor, the student's parent or guardian. The release or disclosure of information is not an act of professional misconduct if

  1. the student (or, if the student is a minor, the student's parent or guardian) consents to the release or disclosure, or

  2. if the release or disclosure is required or allowed by law.

- Abusing a student physically, sexually, verbally, psychologically, or emotionally

- Practicing or purporting to practice the profession while under the influence of any substance or while adversely affected by any dysfunction

  1. which the teacher knows or ought to know impairs the teacher's ability to practice and

  2. for which treatment has previously been recommended, ordered, or prescribed but the teacher has failed to follow the treatment

- Failing to keep records as required by his or her professional duties

- Failing to supervise adequately a person who is under the professional supervision of the teacher

- Falsifying a record relating to the teacher's professional responsibilities

- Contravening a law if the contravention has caused or may cause a student who is under the teacher's professional supervision to be put at or to remain at risk

- Conduct unbecoming a teacher

- Failing to take reasonable steps to ensure that requested information is provided in a complete and accurate manner

- Practicing the profession while the teacher is in a conflict of interest

- Failing to comply with duties related to child protection

A Caution Regarding Teacher Discipline

Principals should always assume that any decision to discipline a teacher will result in a grievance by the applicable union.

Principals therefore must satisfy themselves, via direct consultation with their supervisor where possible, that the employer is prepared to defend the decision.

In addition, a fair and thorough investigation and diligent record keeping will be essential in justifying a discipline decision to an arbitrator.

7. Termination of Employment

The termination of a teacher's employment must be accomplished by a district-approved resolution and is generally enacted when the teacher's behavior (on or off duty) is so refractory as to jeopardize the safety and well-being of students or colleagues. Less often, a termination of employment occurs when a teacher fails to improve his performance after a period of focused observation, professional dialogue, time offered to effect improvements in the teaching performance, and extensive documentation.

Termination of employment caused by inappropriate or unacceptable behavior usually, but not always, follows upon a series of disciplinary measures against the teacher; it is rarely the first course of action in such situations, but it can be.

Where either dismissal or termination of a staff member's employment becomes likely, you must seek the advice and assistance of your supervisor.

TIPS

Further Reading

Danielson, C. (1996) *Enhancing Professional Practice: A Framework for Teaching*

Danielson, C., and McGreal, T. (2000) *Teacher Evaluation to Enhance Professional Practice*

Be Visible

Take time to stay connected to students and staff. That is why you are a principal. Visit a classroom every day.

Be in the hall when classes change and they'll think you're everywhere.

The Voice of Experience

Teaching Staff: Selection and Development

→ TEACHING STAFF SELECTION: GETTING STARTED

One of the most significant and rewarding aspects of your job as a principal is hiring new teachers—getting the right person. Decisions you make about teaching assignments when organizing the school are also critical—getting the right person in the right job.

1. When hiring new staff, you will follow a similar selection process whether you are

- looking for one person to fill an immediate vacancy,

- hiring several new staff members in the spring, based on September projections,

- engaging a long-term occasional teacher for a specified period of time.'

2. Review your district's human resources or employee services policies and procedures. These might include the following:

- Teacher hiring

- Posting of vacancies

- Record retention

- Interview protocols

- Application and selection procedures

Review your district's handbook regarding interviewing and hiring new staff.

3. Review the collective agreements related to any selection processes you will be conducting. Collective agreements usually

- set rules governing how new positions or vacancies are to be filled,

- mandate requirements for job postings,

- establish district staffing timelines for interviewing and making selection decisions.

4. Find out who at the district office is responsible, within each employee group, for staffing and the administration of the collective agreement. Introduce yourself to these people. Begin to build a positive working relationship with the personnel officer responsible for academic staffing as soon as possible. Don't hesitate to ask for advice and assistance.

INTERVIEWING AND HIRING

The Process

1. Identify your staffing needs.

2. Get authority to post the vacant or new position. Some districts hire from a pool; you will then be interviewing and selecting teachers from the pool the district has already hired.

3. Follow the district's staffing timelines and procedures.

4. Form an interview committee according to the procedures (e.g., the committee may include you, the vice-principal, off-site personnel, or some combination of these or other personnel).

5. Develop a candidate profile, including information such as
   - qualifications required;
   - internal candidates only, or external as well;
   - seniority provisions (e.g., candidate must be on a full-time, not part-time, contract with the district);
   - bilingualism required.

6. Post the vacancy according to district procedures.

7. Follow a standardized application process, according to district procedures.
   - Inform office staff about the staffing details so they can answer inquiries.
   - Create a log sheet or information sheet to be used when speaking to applicants on the phone.
   - Determine whether applications will be received by fax; prepare for a possible deluge.

8. Screen the applications for an interview short list.
   - Develop a one-page summary form for use when reviewing and screening applications.
   - Ensure that candidates are in good standing and have the necessary qualifications.

9. Develop interview questions.
   - Start with a standardized job description.
   - Establish a hierarchy of selection criteria.
   - Develop questions designed to elicit information about desired skills and knowledge.
   - Rehearse members of the interview committee.

10. Provide all members of the interview committee with relevant information regarding the competition.
    - Decide which questions each will ask.
    - Assign a scribe or have each member take notes.

- One interviewer should always be fully attentive to the response rather than engaged in writing.

11. Develop an interview schedule.

    - Determine how long the interviews will be and where they will be conducted.

    - Schedule a few minutes breathing space between interviews.

12. Conduct interviews following a standardized process; equity demands equal conditions.

    - Use a consistent set of questions asked by the same committee members each time.

    - Ask follow-up or probing questions when appropriate.

    - Stick to the scheduled length of time for each interview.

13. Consider a second round of interviews if no candidate is satisfactory; usually you will not need to do so.

14. Keep all records of the selection process and interviews.

    - Notes taken during the interviews should be objective and reflect what was said.

    - File and retain these records according to district procedure.

15. Check your preferred candidates' references; follow your district protocol if one exists.

    - Checking references is a critical stage in the selection process; don't leave it out.

16. Make the recommendation to hire; follow district procedures.

    - Some districts require the interviewer to submit the top two or three candidates; then the district makes the final selection on behalf of the school.

17. Complete any additional paper work required by the human resources department in your district.

18. Remember, if your first-choice candidate declines the job, you need to have a Plan B.

19. Notify all the unsuccessful applicants yourself as quickly as possible; prepare a statement to use in these conversations so that you will cover all necessary information.

20. Announce the names of successful candidates to the staff and other stakeholders.

21. Invite new staff members to the school for a welcome and initial orientation session.

    • Make sure the orientation for new staff is not limited to a one-day event.

    • Provide for ongoing support for new staff in your school's staff development plan.

What Do You Do When You Have No Qualified Candidates?

Network with your principal colleagues; they may know of suitable candidates. If you have no one, call your supervisor and district human resources department for advice.

> Effective principals hire and retain high quality teachers and hold them responsible for student learning.
>
> —*Leading Learning Communities: Standards for What Principals Should Know and Be Able to Do,* National Association of Elementary School Principals

→ TEACHING STAFF DEVELOPMENT: GETTING STARTED

> Staff development, professional development, professional growth, professional learning: The ultimate goal of all of these is to improve instruction and thus improve student achievement.

TIPS

As principal, your staff development role at the school has many facets, including

• Working with staff to identify their professional needs

• Planning, organizing, and facilitating staff development programs that

Improve staff effectiveness

Are consistent with school goals and needs

- Supervising both individuals and groups

- Providing feedback on performance

- Arranging for remedial assistance for individuals as needed

- Engaging staff and others to plan and participate in staff development activities

- Initiating your own professional development

SOURCE: *Principals for Our Changing Schools: The Knowledge and Skill Base*, S. D. Thompson, p. 11-3.

1. School Staff Development Plan

Review the following:

- Human resources policies and procedures relating to staff development

- District's handbook on staff supervision and professional growth

- School's staff development plan (update in consultation with staff)

- Relevant collective agreement clauses

The staff development plan may include the following:

- An overall focus, significant goals, and specific objectives

- Responsibility centers and timelines

- Strategies to encourage staff participation

- Resources available, including time and money

- A list (and schedule) of planned staff development activities

- Supports available as follow-up to these activities (e.g., mentoring and coaching)

- A process to assess the results and impact of the staff development activities

- A procedure for evaluating and modifying the staff development plan itself

The staff development plan will be linked to the data driven school improvement plan or districtwide priorities, such as the following:

- Curriculum knowledge
- Student assessment
- Special education
- Teaching strategies
- Classroom management and leadership
- Use of technology
- Communicating with parents and students

2. District and External Resources

Find out which district personnel are responsible for staff development and curriculum support. Introduce yourself and find out how they can assist you with the staff development program at your school. Get a copy of the district's professional development calendar. Apprise yourself of professional development projects that may be available through the local university, college, or professional association.

3. Staff Participation

Invite teachers at the school to make presentations to staff on topics of interest to peers. Look for ways to provide presenters with time to prepare. Seek input from staff as to the best format, location, and time for these sessions. Check collective agreements for any related provisions.

Consider a staff development component for staff meetings. These regular presentations can be given by invited guests, staff members, or representatives from the district office. Be sure to prepare and present some of these staff development sessions yourself.

Consult staff on how to make best use of in-school professional activity days, if you have any.

4. New Staff

Provide orientation programs for all new staff members, including beginning and experienced teachers and nonteaching staff.

Provide new staff with a comprehensive staff handbook. Invite staff members to help update the staff handbook annually. This is an excellent professional development opportunity for interested individuals.

Develop an ongoing plan for supporting beginning teachers. This might include

- regular information and discussion sessions dealing with anticipated activities (e.g., the first day of school, parent-teacher interviews, completing the state or district report card, developing professional growth plans and portfolios);

- individual coaching for each beginning teacher through a mentoring relationship with an experienced teacher in the school (see Part V for further information);

- mentor teachers who are interested in further career development beyond the classroom.

5. Principal Professional Development

Be sure to develop your own professional growth plan for the year; do not neglect yourself.

Share your growth plan with the staff; model your commitment to lifelong learning.

Establish a mentoring relationship for yourself with a more experienced principal.

Get involved in professional associations locally and nationally.

Take advantage of training and information sessions provided by your district.

Remember, you cannot be an expert in everything all at once.

Set a focus for yourself and establish your priorities over a three- to five-year cycle.

See Part V, "Looking After Yourself," for more suggestions concerning your own professional development.

Effective principals provide opportunities for teachers to work, plan, and think together:

- Common planning time: Time and space is set aside for teachers to work together.

- Subject-area or grade-level meetings: Effective principals participate in these meetings.

- Coaching and mentoring: Expert teachers coach new teachers; individuals work with mentors.

SOURCE: Adapted from *Leading Learning Communities: Standards for What Principals Should Know and Be Able to Do*, National Association of Elementary School Principals, pp. 45–50.

⊙ PROFESSIONAL LEARNING

Further Opportunities for Professional Growth: An Overview

Support and encourage staff members as they plan and undertake a variety of professional growth activities. Following is an overview of a wide variety of opportunities available to teachers.

Certificate programs

Academic programs

- Universities and colleges

Professional networks

- Participate on subject councils
- Work with the school advisory groups
- Join informal study or reading groups

Mentoring or coaching

- Serve as an associate teacher
- Mentor a new teacher

Learning through practice

- Develop new curriculum materials
- Conduct action research
- Pilot new initiatives

Research activities

- Plan and conduct research
- Explore ways to access and use educational research

Professional activities

- Visit other educational settings
- Develop a reading list
- Maintain a professional portfolio

Professional contributions

- Present at conferences
- Contribute to professional publications

Technology and learning

- Engage in professional learning using information/communication technology
- Research on the Internet

> Effective staff development practices consider the needs and specific job-related responsibilities of each individual.
>
> —*If I Only Knew*, H. B. Alvy and P. Robbins, p. 163

WORKING WITH BEGINNING TEACHERS

You may have several beginning teachers on staff every year. Working with them both individually and collectively will be a very significant part of your job. Use your district's beginning-teacher induction program in conjunction with your school-based program. If your district does not have a program, encourage the development of one this year.

Invite all new staff members to visit the school for an initial orientation session. Provide all new staff with a comprehensive staff handbook. Plan orientation programs for all new staff members, including beginning and experienced teachers and nonteaching staff. Make sure the orientation for new staff is not limited to a one-day event.

Provide for ongoing support for beginning teachers within your school's staff development plan. Ensure that beginning teachers understand the teacher performance appraisal process.

Design and deliver an induction program to support beginning teachers. This program might include

- regular information and discussion sessions dealing with anticipated activities (e.g., the first day of school, parent-teacher interviews, completing the report card, developing professional growth plans and portfolios);
- individual coaching for each beginning teacher through a mentoring relationship with an experienced teacher in the school.

TIPS

- Let new teachers have first crack at the stockroom. Also, put back the resources that have mysteriously disappeared from their classrooms.

- Ensure that department heads and team leaders have the curriculum resources they need to support the new teachers in their departments and teams.

- Take a look at new teachers' classrooms; look for an opportunity to commend.

- Tell them why they need to be nice to custodians and secretaries.

- Talk to new teachers about early proactive contact with parents and the power of "glad calls."

- Provide support systems for their high profile and high needs students.

- In the third or fourth week of September, spend some quality discussion time with new teachers to find out how their year has started.

- Most important, let them know that NO question is too silly.

Hire well.

Staffing decisions are critical.

If I could give only one piece of advice, it would be to hire well.

— The Voice of Experience —

Professional Relations

WORKING WITH THE UNIONS IN YOUR SCHOOL

Managing in a Union Environment: An Overview

As a principal or vice-principal, you are no longer part of the teachers' union; you are now part of senior administration (i.e., management) and, as such, represent the district. Your responsibility is to ensure that you administer in accordance with all provisions of the collective agreements of the employee groups at the school. You need to know these collective agreements in detail.

Teachers are less likely to share issues and concerns with you than they were when you were a teacher, especially issues related to discontent with your management style. Your influence is solely through the management structure, not through the union.

In some situations, you may be accused of unfair labor practices; for example:

- Undermining legal sanctions
- Using intimidation
- Using threats
- Using undue influence
- Coercion, which can be regarded as antiunion or interfering in the formation, selection, or administration of a trade union or the representation of employees by a trade union

As principals and vice-principals, you and your colleagues may

- serve as management representatives on labor-management committees,
- participate in district meetings and district committee meetings without obligations to unions,
- supervise and discipline staff solely from a management perspective,
- be involved in tasks on behalf of senior management,
- have significant increases in responsibilities.

➔ Building and Maintaining Positive Relationships: Getting Started

1. Treat the unions with respect.

   Invite union representatives to provide items for the staff meeting agenda and joint committees.

   Respect unions and their rights under collective agreements.

   Invite union representation to attend meetings with individual staff members when discipline is contemplated.

   Understand the role of the union stewards and branch presidents and facilitate their roles; for example, support collective agreement provisions for time off to conduct union business, subject to the need to leave lesson plans for classes.

   Do not personalize collective agreement disputes, especially grievances.

2. Recognize that you are part of the management team.

   Be professional and collaborative with those you supervise.

   Understand thoroughly all collective agreements; it is your duty to administer them.

Support management's perspective on all collective agreements.

Find out which of your colleagues, and which district office employees, have expertise to offer in the area of labor relations; know when to seek their advice and assistance.

Work with your colleagues to encourage the district to

- consult school administrators regarding bargaining and the ongoing review of collective agreements and

- provide training regarding collective agreements and union relations to district supervisory officers and school administrators together.

3. Continue to work toward developing a collaborative culture with staff.

Explain to the school staff that the district mandates the legal obligations that you must enact.

Continue to solicit staff input and feedback.

Take training in problem-solving, conflict resolution, negotiation, and political management.

> The entire school staff is interdependent.
>
> Its members must rely on each other and be able to resolve their differences.
>
> There are too many pressures on educators today to allow staff-principal conflicts to erode the professional harmony that is a basic necessity in every effective school.

→ COLLECTIVE AGREEMENTS AND GRIEVANCES

Collective Agreements: Getting Started

1. **Identify** which unions operate in your school. Meet with the union stewards in your school. Invite them to brief you. Find out who the branch presidents are for your district. Record their names and phone numbers. Introduce yourself. Find out who administers each of the collective agreements at the district office and introduce yourself.

2. **Review** current copies of every collective agreement in force in your school. Keep a copy of each collective agreement at school and another

at home for quick reference. Collective agreements clarify required actions for both parties in an effort to promote fairness and consistency. Collective agreements usually address matters that include the following:

- Salary and grids

- Allowances

- Leaves

- Benefits and gratuities

- Staffing and staffing committees

- Seniority

- Working conditions (e.g., allocation of instructional and noninstructional time, parameters for supervision of students, health and safety)

- Staff evaluation

- Grievances and arbitration

⊜ Grievances: An Overview

Grievances are generally defined in collective agreements as a difference between the parties related to the interpretation, application, or administration of the contract. Disputes arising from collective agreements are to be resolved through arbitration. Grievances of individuals are usually brought forward by their union on their behalf. There are four broad types of grievances:

- Individual grievances (the type you are most likely to encounter at your school)

- Group grievances

- Policy grievances

- Policy/individual grievances

The grievance process usually includes three or four steps:

1. Pregrievance discussion

2. Initiating the grievance

3. Pre-arbitration (Often there are two steps seeking resolution before arbitration, usually involving the principal and then the superintendent.)

4. Arbitration (This could involve an arbitrator or an arbitration panel.)

1. **Check** your district policy and individual collective agreements for details concerning each specific grievance process. Timelines will be set out; both parties must adhere to them.

2. **Be aware** that grievances may be brought forward regarding the discipline or dismissal of a union member. Grievance arbitration is now the only way to contest the dismissal or termination of a teacher.

3. **Discuss** the situation with your supervisor if you believe you are headed toward a grievance.

Strategies to Assist Principals With Collective Agreements and Grievances

Be fair and reasonable. Be aware that your actions and decisions can be grieved.

Recognize the professional experience to be gained through grievance and arbitration.

Document; maintain confidential files securely.

Discuss collective agreement issues with your supervisor and human resources department first.

In the event of job action, such as a strike, you and the vice-principal are the frontline representatives of district management. You owe a duty of honesty, fairness, and loyalty to the district, and only the district. You should not make any statement or take any actions that could be construed or perceived as being contrary to the interests of the district.

Follow district policy. Where there appears to be no policy or protocol, seek direction from the district office. As a district representative you have a duty to seek and carry out the district's instruction. Where those instructions are given verbally, request written confirmation. If the district issues contingency plans and policies for the operation of the school during the job action, you must implement them in good faith, as part of the performance of your employment contract.

If you have questions about how to handle disruptions at your school during a job action, speak to your supervisor.

Be Prepared

Read and understand the collective agreements.

Keep organized. Handle paper once. Have files and make binders.

The Voice of Experience

Celebrating Success

GETTING STARTED

Effective principals honor and recognize those who have worked to serve students and the purpose of the school.

—How leaders influence the culture
of schools, K. D. Peterson and T. E. Deal,
Educational Leadership, 56(1), p. 30

Celebrating the accomplishments of students, parents, and staff is an important component of your role as principal. Celebrations are one way to foster a positive school culture—and school culture is a significant factor in student motivation and achievement and in teacher work satisfaction and productivity. Here are some suggestions for getting started.

1. Know and be able to articulate your own values and beliefs about learning and teaching, and about how students and teachers should be recognized and rewarded. Be aware of valued rewards.

2. Understand and respect the traditions and history, heroes and heroines, symbols and ceremonies at your new school—"the way we do things here." It is important to get to know the school's culture as quickly as possible.

3. Determine whether there are identifiable subcultures or subgroups of students, staff, and families in the school.

Shaping School Culture

It is up to school leaders—principals, teachers, and often parents—to help identify, shape and maintain strong, positive, student-focused cultures.

—How leaders influence the culture
of schools, K. D. Peterson and T. E. Deal,
Educational Leadership, 56(1), p. 28

---

4. Assess your school against the following school culture norms, which need to be strong in order to create a healthy school.

a. Collegiality
b. Experimentation
c. High expectations
d. Trust and confidence
e. Tangible support
f. Reaching out to the knowledge base
g. Appreciation and recognition
h. Caring, celebration, and humor
i. Involvement in decision-making
j. Protection of what's important
k. Traditions
l. Honest, open communication

SOURCE: Good seeds grow in strong cultures, J. Saphier and M. King, *Educational Leadership*, 42(6), pp. 67–74.

5. Acknowledge that there are unique cultural differences in each school. Each school will respond differently to change; staff and students will react differently to appreciation and recognition.

6. Help the school community focus on the students; begin by telling the stories (past and present) of their accomplishments and achievements.

7. Consider which policies and programs (instructional and coinstructional) support an emotionally healthy school.

8. Determine what elements of the culture are standing in the way of the success of students, staff, and parents, and how to move away from those elements without alienating stakeholders.

9. Discuss your findings and observations about school culture and celebrating success with principal colleagues, a mentor, the superintendent, and the vice-principal if you have one.

10. Don't try to change things too quickly at your new school. Observe, listen, and learn.

> Recognition is a cure for many ills.
>
> —*The Essential John Nash*, H. W. Kuhn and S. Nasar, Eds., p. vii

CREATING AN ENVIRONMENT FOR SUCCESS

Model the Behavior You Want Others to Exhibit

- Focus your energies on success.
- Be optimistic, respectful, and thoughtful.
- Share time, skills, ideas, and resources.
- Engage in conversations about teaching and learning.
- Be humble and learn from others by listening and observing.
- Ask for ideas, help, and volunteers.
- Request feedback on your performance.
- Attend student assemblies, sporting events, concerts, dramatic presentations, etc.

- Analyze the ways in which motivation works; talk about motivation with staff, students, and parents.

- Encourage positive relationships and open communication with parents.

Expect the Best

- Articulate clearly school standards and goals.

- Welcome staff and students into the building each day.

- Catch people doing something right.

- Look for examples of best practice.

- Ensure that appropriate time, support, and resources are available to design and implement a ceremony or special event.

- Make role models of former students, community members, and nationally known personalities.

- Encourage staff, students, and parents to be proud of great work.

Design a Rewards and Recognition Program

- Reward students and staff for attaining their personal best.

- Recognize the variety of ways students and staff can be successful.

- Provide performance feedback on an ongoing basis.

- Look for ways to provide positive feedback to staff and students.

- Ensure that every student has at least one adult advocate in the school.

- Honor the need for choice and control.

- Celebrate accomplishments of former students and staff.

- Keep a file of recognition ideas.

- Write thank you notes.

- E-mail positive comments about a classroom visit.

- Create a principal's recognition event honoring students.

- Have an end-of-year awards assembly.

- Have private as well as public rewards and recognition.
- Involve the school advisory group, student council, and staff in designing a recognition program.

Keep in mind that different people react differently to public recognition. Also, be sensitive to jealousies that can arise among staff or students in response to public praise.

Link Rewards and Praise to Standards and Values

- Insist on courtesy and respect from staff, students, parents, and visitors to the school.
- Phone or write parents or guardians when a student has met a goal or reached a milestone.
- Ask the students about their learning during a classroom visit.
- Talk with the students about their dreams and goals.
- Acknowledge and honor existing school traditions.
- Design new traditions and ceremonies that reflect changing beliefs and values.
- Ensure celebrations reflect the traditions of all cultures and religions represented in the school community.
- Include all students.
- Balance competition with cooperation.
- Create opportunities for staff to get together professionally and socially.

SHARING SUCCESS

Schedule Celebrations

- Have assemblies featuring student performances and awards.
- Host recognition events for volunteers, bus drivers, and cafeteria staff.
- Celebrate heroes and heroines whose behavior exemplifies the school's core values.

- Invite staff, parents, and members of the community to challenge the students to a sports activity.

- Celebrate staff and student accomplishments.

TIPS Your supervisor may appreciate being kept informed about the accomplishments of students and staff at your school. Pass along the good news.

Recognize Milestones, Transitions, and Changes

- Host a school anniversary reunion.

- Plan special events to mark a school closure.

- Take time to explain why you made certain decisions.

- Share information about district policies; help students, staff, and parents understand the requirements.

- When dealing with a tragedy, access the district's tragic events team.

Link Students and Staff With the World Outside of School

- Twin with another school to promote cultural understanding.

- Adopt a community service or charity.

- Design a school Web site.

- Promote international exchanges for both students and teachers.

- Invite students and teachers from other states and countries for a study or work term.

- Create a tutor or literacy program using seniors or students from the local high school.

At the elementary level, children are likely to receive three negative comments for every positive comment they hear. By middle school, the ratio jumps to nine negative comments for every positive communication. And by high school, kids might hear between eleven and seventeen criticisms before they hear one bit of encouragement.

—*Creating Emotionally Safe Schools: A Guide forEducators and Parents*, J. Bluestein, p. 134

Consciously Build a Positive School Culture

- Promote dialogue about teaching and learning.

- Provide positive feedback to staff and students when change occurs.

- Foster collaborative decision making.

- Be sure to take issues of adult learning, teacher overload, and staff burnout seriously.

- Ensure that staff is aware of any district employee assistance program.

- Offer leadership training to students as well as staff.

- Invite groups of students to your office for conversations on topics of their choice.

- Start small and celebrate each success.

NEGATIVE ENVIRONMENTS

Some of the indicators of a negative environment are blaming, lack of communication, impatience, a heavy reliance on rules and punishment, individualism rather than collegiality, high crime and dropout rates, poor building maintenance, rising school suspensions, and decreasing academic achievement.

> Some schools develop "toxic" cultures, which actively discourage efforts to improve teaching or student achievement.
>
> —Time use flows from school culture:
> River of values and traditions can
> nurture or poison staff development,
> K. D. Peterson, *Journal of Staff Development*, 20(2)

If you find yourself in a school with a negative environment, consider the following suggestions:

1. Based on the collaborative decision-making process, develop a school improvement plan with measurable outcomes, timelines, and responsibility centers.

2. Share the action plan with all the stakeholders including, on some occasions, the media.

3. Monitor the implementation of the improvement plan; give recognition, praise, and support to staff, students, and parents who are contributing to meeting the goals.

4. Evaluate and revise your plan.

5. Celebrate the success of staff, students, parents, and community, and share that success.

Further Reading Regarding School Culture

Peterson, K. D., and Deal, T. E. (2002) *The Shaping of School Culture Fieldbook*

Value Staff

Never lose sight of the fact that you were once a teacher.

Look for lots of ways to appreciate and recognize the efforts of staff. Look in the shadows for those efforts that often go unnoticed.

Always keep in mind that the single most important characteristic of a highly successful classroom is the high morale of the teacher.

The Voice of Experience

PART III

Behavior and Discipline

Student Behavior and Discipline in the School

→ GETTING STARTED

1. District and School Codes of Conduct

Know the school district's policies and procedures on behavior and discipline and the police and district protocol. (See Chapter 22, "Student Behavior and Outside Agencies," for further information regarding police and school protocols.)

Review the district and school codes of conduct to ensure consistency.

2. Communicating Expectations

Ensure that the school code of conduct is communicated to students and parents at the start of the school year and on an ongoing basis. Students and parents need to know in advance that suspension and expulsion may be the consequence of misconduct. Discuss district and school codes of conduct regularly with school staff. Provide support and information to new and occasional staff. Discuss only general issues regarding student behavior, discipline, and safety at school advisory group meetings throughout the year. Do not discuss individuals. Solicit the views of the school advisory group regarding the local code of conduct and school policies or guidelines concerning the appropriate dress of pupils.

3. Principal and Vice-Principal Duties

Consult with the vice-principal (if there is one) on student behavior and discipline. Clarify the roles you and the vice-principal will assume consistent with district policy. Keep in mind that the principal is ultimately responsible for discipline. If you delegate supervisory authority to the vice-principal, be sure to maintain adequate communication and supervision. The following actions are recommended:

- Establish an open door policy.
- Implement a regular reporting structure on delegated responsibilities.
- Communicate frequently and regularly about students, staff, and other issues.
- All serious issues should be reported directly to the principal regardless of any general delegation of authority.

4. Shared Responsibilities

Include other staff members involved in monitoring and supporting student behavior. Involve them in discussions and role clarification. Meet with members of the special education resource team; for example, psychiatrists, social workers, and psychologists. Clarify their roles and responsibilities in working with students, parents, and staff. Begin immediately to build positive relationships with all parents, especially those of students experiencing ongoing difficulty.

5. Documentation

Document factually all interviews, incidents, meetings, and phone calls regarding student behavior and discipline. Record the time, date, place, participants, and what was said. File your documentation. Establish a system, electronic or otherwise, for filing notes regarding contacts with students and parents. Ensure that both principal and vice-principal have access to these notes and follow the same record keeping system. Keep all records secure.

Remember that notes may be subject to subpoena. Be factual.

6. Support Programs

Find out about available school programs, preventative measures, and routines that promote a safe environment and a positive atmosphere; for example:

- Violence prevention programs integrated into the curriculum at each grade level

- Conflict resolution, peer mediation, and student crime-stopper programs

- Strategies to improve students' self-esteem and social and communication skills

- Programs to encourage student participation in school activities

- Early identification and intervention strategies

- Counseling or mentoring for at-risk students

See Chapter 23: "Protecting Our Students."

TIPS

Practice scheduled visibility.

Plan to be visible around and about the school each day. Your presence will help to set the tone in the school and reduce incidents of student misconduct.

DISTRICT POLICIES AND PROCEDURES: AN OVERVIEW

Behavior, Discipline, and Safety

Follow your district's policies and procedures regarding student behavior, discipline, and safety. Among others, these policies and procedures might include the following titles:

- Safe Schools

- Code of Conduct

- Student Suspension and Suspension Hearing Panel

- Student Expulsion and Expulsion Hearing Panel

- Critical Incident Review

- Withdrawal of Transportation Privileges
- Substance Abuse
- Weapons
- Access to School Sites
- Police and District Protocol
- Search and Seizure
- Crisis Response Plan
- Tragic Events Team

Suspension Procedures

School district procedures regarding student suspensions will cover the following topics:

- Mandatory and discretionary reasons for suspension
- Procedures to follow
- Mitigating factors
- Notification of a suspension
- Maintenance of record in student file
- Review of a suspension
- Sample notification letters to be used

Suspension of a Pupil

A pupil *may* be suspended from his or her school and from engaging in all school-related activities if the pupil commits any of the following infractions while he or she is at school or is engaged in a school-related activity:

1. Uttering a threat to inflict serious bodily harm on another person

2. Possessing alcohol or illegal drugs

3. Being under the influence of alcohol

4. Swearing at a teacher or at another person in a position of authority

5. Committing an act of vandalism that causes extensive damage to school property at the pupil's school or to property located on the premises of the pupil's school

6. Engaging in another activity that, under a policy of the district, is one for which a suspension is mandatory

Expulsion Procedures

School district procedures regarding student expulsions may cover the following topics:

- Definitions of limited and full expulsion
- Mandatory and discretionary reasons for expulsion
- Procedures to follow
- Suspension pending expulsion
- Mitigating factors
- Principal's inquiry leading to expulsion and principal's determination
- Duration of expulsion
- Notification of expulsion
- Appeal of an expulsion
- Return from expulsion
- Sample notification letters to be used

Expulsion of a Pupil

A pupil *may* be expelled if the pupil commits any of the following infractions while he or she is at school or is engaged in a school-related activity:

1. Possessing a weapon, including possessing a firearm

2. Using a weapon to cause or to threaten bodily harm to another person

3. Committing physical assault on another person that causes bodily harm requiring treatment by a medical practitioner

4. Committing sexual assault

5. Trafficking in weapons or in illegal drugs

6. Committing robbery

7. Giving alcohol to a minor

8. Engaging in another activity that, under a policy of the district school board, is one for which expulsion is mandatory

Follow your district's policies and procedures in all matters related to suspension and expulsion. Most jurisdictions have safe-schools legislation that defines the regulations around suspensions and expulsions.

BEHAVIOR CODES

Be sure to follow your district's policies and procedures regarding school codes of conduct and dress codes. Remember, principals should solicit the views of the school advisory group regarding both the local code of conduct and school policies and guidelines concerning appropriate dress of pupils.

Codes of Conduct

The purpose of a code of conduct is to set the stage for managing the behavior of all persons on school premises.

Sample Code of Conduct

Guiding Principles

- All participants involved in the school system—students, parents or guardians, volunteers, teachers, and other staff members—are included in this Code of Conduct whether they are on school property, on school buses, or at school-authorized events or activities.

- All members of the school community are to be treated with respect and dignity, especially persons in positions of authority.

- Responsible citizenship involves appropriate participation in the civic life of the school community. Active and engaged citizens are aware of their rights, but more important, they accept responsibility for protecting their rights and the rights of others.

- Members of the school community are expected to use nonviolent means to resolve conflict. Physically aggressive behavior is not a responsible way to interact with others.

- The possession, use, or threatened use of any object to injure another person endangers the safety of oneself and others.

- Alcohol and illegal drugs are addictive and present a health hazard. Schools will work cooperatively with police and drug and alcohol agencies to promote prevention strategies and, where necessary, respond to school members who are in possession of, or under the influence of, alcohol or illegal drugs.

- Insults, disrespect, and other hurtful acts disrupt learning and teaching in a school community. Members of the school community have a responsibility to maintain an environment where conflict and difference can be addressed in a manner characterized by respect and civility.

Dress Codes

The successful enforcement of the school dress code requires both an understanding of the school and community culture and the application of common sense and sound judgment. Follow the district policy on developing a dress code.

ACCESS TO SCHOOL PREMISES

Follow the district's policies and procedures regarding access to school premises. There will be explicit directions and form letters to use. Always consult with the superintendent when contemplating the limiting of access or issuing a trespass letter. Principals have the power to exclude anyone from the school whose presence is detrimental to pupils.

Document

Document all conversations with parents, teachers, and students.

Don't jump to conclusions. Check out the story with students and staff before making decisions. Keep written notes on all incidents.

Always document factually, objectively, dispassionately, and truthfully. It will save you hours of agonizing later when you try to remember.

The Voice of Experience

Student Behavior and Outside Agencies

At a Glance

- Police/School Protocol
- Search and Seizure
    An Overview
    When Will a Search Be Lawful?
- The Young Offender
    Implications for the School
- School Attendance
    An Overview
    Getting Started

POLICE/SCHOOL PROTOCOL

Review the district's police/school protocol and any related policies and procedures. A district's protocol may cover the 20 required elements noted below:

1. Role and mandate of police services

2. Role and mandate of school districts

3. Definitions and explanations of terms

4. Occurrences requiring police involvement or response (This list may include, at a minimum, physical assault causing bodily harm requiring medical attention, sexual assault, robbery, criminal harassment, and drug offenses.)

5. Other occurrences requiring police involvement or response (This list may include hate- and bias-motivated incidents, gang-related incidents, extortion, threats of serious physical injury, incidents of vandalism, and trespassing incidents.)

6. Information sharing and disclosure

7. School reporting procedures

8. Police contact information

9. Investigating school incidents
   a. Legal rights
   b. Search and seizure
   c. Detention and arrest
   d. Victim's assistance

10. Police interviews of students
    a. Notification of parents
    b. Preparation for interviews
    c. Conduct of interviews

11. Reporting of children suspected to be in need of protection

12. Investigations involving students with special needs

13. Occurrences involving children under the age of 12

14. School district communication strategy

15. Protocol evaluation process

16. Nonincident-related police involvement

17. Violence prevention programs

18. Physical safety issues

19. Risk assessment services

20. Emergency and crisis response plan

TIPS Your district's police/school protocol is the one you must follow.

SEARCH AND SEIZURE

⊙ An Overview

A search of a student, or of a student's locker or desk, should be done only when permitted by district policy and should be carried out in accordance with the policy. The district policy should indicate if and when police should be contacted. If you do proceed with a search, keep in mind the following:

- You must have reasonable grounds to believe that a breach of school regulations has occurred.
- The search must be authorized by legislation.
- The search must be reasonable, not invasive.
- You must not act as an agent of the police (i.e., school discipline, not criminal charges, must be the primary motivation for the search).

When Will a Search Be Lawful?

Two key questions:

1. When will a search of a student's locker or desk be lawful?
2. When will a personal search of a student be lawful?

In response to these questions, points of law and practical advice are presented, including the comments noted below:

A principal has a duty to search a student, or a student's locker or desk, where it is necessary in order for the principal to fulfill his or her duty to maintain proper order and discipline in the school.

A search warrant is not essential for a search of a student by a school authority.

A principal must have reasonable grounds to believe there was a breach of school regulations or discipline and that a search of the student would reveal evidence of that breach.

THE YOUNG OFFENDER

Implications for the School

1. Governance

Remember that police response will be in accordance with the district's police/school protocol. Outcomes will vary depending on the student's age.

TIPS

> The principal is responsible for maintaining order and discipline; the police are responsible for enforcing the criminal code.

2. Record Keeping

Confidential information about young offenders may be disclosed to school representatives where necessary to ensure compliance of the young person with an authorization or court order, or to ensure the safety of staff, students, or other persons. No person to whom this information is disclosed may disclose it to anyone else unless disclosure is necessary to ensure compliance or safety. The information must be kept separate from other records, be kept confidential, and be destroyed when no longer needed for the reason it was disclosed.

SCHOOL ATTENDANCE

An Overview

School attendance is an issue of student behavior, but it is not necessarily a question of student discipline. The concern arises when parents refuse to send their child to school, or the student refuses to attend school. Chronic or habitual absence generally has a number of underlying causes. The best strategy is to deal immediately with any signs of tardiness, irregular attendance, poor academic performance, or other signs of individual concern. In some communities there may be cultural patterns and historical factors at work as well.

> "How can I maintain attendance at school when I don't know where I am spending the night?"
>
> —*Youth Homelessness in Thunder Bay, A Snap Shot*,
> YES Employment Services

Getting Started

1. District Policy

Review the district's policies and procedures regarding student attendance. Review relevant legislation to be sure of your responsibilities for enforcing school attendance, if this is a significant issue at the school.

2. School Practice

Review the school's current prevention and intervention strategies for promoting, tracking, monitoring, and reporting school attendance. Determine whether you are dealing with one or two individual instances of chronic absence, or a pattern of habitual absence of several students at the school. Plan your follow-up strategies accordingly; you may need to develop a systemic response if the latter is the case.

3. Staff Participation

Review with teachers any concerns or suggestions they have regarding student attendance. Discuss student assessment and evaluation practices in general, and the assessment and evaluation of frequently absent students in particular. Form a staff committee to review school attendance and develop or revise the school plan. Involve others as appropriate.

Review all school policies, procedures, and practices concerning attendance. These might include a safe arrival program (elementary); reporting of absences to parents; expectations regarding vacations, appointments, and other out-of-school activities during regular school hours; consequences for unexcused absences; and expectations of students regarding instruction and assignments they missed during an absence.

4. Consultation

Investigate what strategies are being used by schools facing similar circumstances. Discuss school attendance at school advisory group meetings. Do not discuss individual or identifiable cases.

Seek input and assistance from community organizations and agencies. Clarify the roles played by

- the school district attendance counselor if there is one,

- social workers,

- psychologists,

- a child protection agency (in individual cases).

Acquaint yourself with district policies and procedures regarding home instruction and other accommodations for long-term illness, homeschooling, and supervised alternative learning for excused pupils of compulsory school age.

5. Dealing With Individual Cases

Ensure that the student and parents clearly understand their obligations and responsibilities regarding compulsory school attendance. Inquire about any specific reasons for the habitual absence of an individual student. Provide supports (including counseling) for individual students and parents through school staff and district office staff (e.g., a social worker). Determine whether there is a need for special education or other program supports.

Be Prepared

Be prepared. The day is never as you planned it.

Remember, the interruptions ARE the job.

The Voice of Experience

PART IV

Health and Safety

Protecting Our Students

At a Glance

- Getting Started
- Issues Concerning At-Risk Children and Youth
    - *Access to Information About Students*
    - *Reporting Suspected Child Abuse and Neglect*
    - *Alleged Misconduct or Harassment by School Employees or Volunteers Toward a Student*
    - *Using Reasonable Force for Corrective Purposes*
    - *Missing and Abducted Children*
    - *The Rights of Noncustodial Parents*
    - *Bullying*
    - *Suicide Intervention*
    - *Homeless Children and Youth*

GETTING STARTED

This chapter provides a very brief overview of a number of critical issues concerning at-risk children and youth. You will want to examine each of these topics in greater detail, within the context of your own school setting. Please note that the list of topics presented here is not exhaustive.

1. Follow your district's policies, procedures, and protocols governing the protection of students. Ensure that school procedures comply with district policies. Educate staff about their responsibilities and expected behaviors regarding protecting students.

2. Respect partnerships and protocols developed by the district for working with community agencies such as a child protection agency, probation officers, community resource center social workers, the police, homeless shelters, and women's shelters.

3. If there is a particular concern at the school (e.g., bullying, significant child poverty), speak about the problem respectfully and honestly with all stakeholders. Keep protection of privacy in mind. Ensure privacy and protection for victims. Begin to seek healing for the victims and the school community; access support from district personnel. Develop plans for long-term solutions.

ISSUES CONCERNING AT-RISK CHILDREN AND YOUTH

Access to Information About Students

Except for the right of the student (and the parent or guardian if a student is under the age of 18 years) to examine the student's record, such information is confidential. When the student reaches the age of 18 years, the parent or guardian has no right to information about the student without the student's permission. In this case, use a consent-to-release information form.

If student information is required by the courts, consult district policy and your supervisor on how that information should be delivered.

Be mindful of your responsibility to control newspaper, radio, and television access to students and to information about students. Follow district protocols regarding the publication of students' names and photos, the use of students' names on publicly displayed work, and other matters related to access to information about students.

Reporting Suspected Child Abuse and Neglect

TIPS

This is a critical aspect of your legal responsibilities; be sure that you thoroughly understand and carefully follow all district policies and procedures in this area.

What to Report and When

If a person has reasonable grounds to suspect that a child has suffered harm or there is a risk that the child may suffer harm, the person must report the suspicion and the information on which it is based to a society, even when the information is discovered in a confidential manner. Further reports must be made if additional information is discovered. Read your district's protocol for child abuse thoroughly. Flag the section with the procedures and have it on hand at all times.

Alleged Misconduct or Harassment by Employees or Volunteers Toward a Student

> Schools are intended to be healthy and nurturing environments within which children can safely grow and learn.
>
> When a school environment is poisoned by sexual crimes or harassment, it is of fundamental concern to us all.
>
> —*Protecting Our Students:*
> *Executive Summary and Recommendations,*
> S. L. Robins, p. 1

In the case of alleged misconduct or harassment by employees or volunteer towards a student, follow your district's policies and procedures. These may include procedures with titles such as Alleged Employee Misconduct Toward a Student and Alleged Harassment.

> Follow all district policies and procedures related to harassment, human rights, etc.

TIPS

When dealing with a situation of alleged misconduct or harassment, consult your supervisor and your professional association.

Using Reasonable Force for Corrective Purposes

No school policy permits strapping, hitting, or other physical punishment for children or teenagers. Staff should be trained in age-appropriate discipline practices.

There may be instances in which a teacher (or a parent) is justified in using reasonable force to correct the behavior of a child. The law permits reasonable force for corrective purposes, but the actions must be reasonable in the circumstances, taking into account the child's age, physical stature, and level of maturity; the nature of the misbehavior; the method and severity of the punishment; and any resulting injury to the child.

Follow your district's policies and procedures governing the use of restraints with students. In some cases districts require parents whose children have been identified as having behavioral issues to sign an agreement permitting school staff to use restraints with the child, in accordance with district policy. Ensure proper training for staff who are likely to be required to restrain students in the course of their duties.

Document any use of force against students, for example, physically restraining a student from hitting another student by grabbing the child's arm (to stop the hit and preserve the safety of the other student).

Uses of force that go beyond what is "reasonable" or that become the subject of a complaint by a parent or guardian ought to be reported to a child protection agency.

Missing and Abducted Children

Prevention Strategies

1. Ensure that trusted adults always supervise the schoolyard and field trips. Insist that school visitors and volunteers be identified with badges. Visitors must sign in. Follow your district requirements for criminal background checks for staff and volunteers.

2. Instruct students to report to an adult supervisor or go to the office if a stranger approaches them on the school grounds or in the school. Provide streetproofing instruction to children and teenagers on a regular basis.

3. Instruct parents and guardians to call the attendance line in advance of a student absence. Call parents or guardians as soon as it is discovered that a student is missing from school without prior notification. Follow your district's policy regarding a safe arrival program.

Do not permit students to leave school with an adult other than the student's parent or a prearranged, responsible caregiver. If the person insists on taking the child, request confirmation from the custodial parent. Ensure that all parents and guardians sign students out when leaving the school and sign students in when arriving at school during the day. All students must sign in and out if unaccompanied.

4. Alert the police regarding strangers in the school or on the grounds, or regarding vehicles that are parked next to the school or in the school parking lot for no apparent reason. Record the make, model, and license plate number of the vehicle. Notify other schools in the area and the district of any concerns.

5. Do not post pictures of children except in compliance with district policy. See Chapter 5, "Communication," and Chapter 9, "Records and Information Management," for further information regarding publication, protection of privacy, and student safety. Link the school's Web site to other sites which offer information to parents and guardians about prevention and protection strategies for children.

When a Student Is Missing

Check the school. Call parents/guardians.

The first 24 hours are critical to the safe return of the child.

Call the police: Describe the student's clothing, location last seen, and possible route taken.

Obtain names of witnesses.

Inform your supervisor.

The Rights of Noncustodial Parents

Alerts

Alert office staff and teachers if there are concerns that a noncustodial parent without access rights will attempt to see the child or obtain information about the child. Use photos of the student and/or the parent to assist staff in identifying persons of concern. File court orders and other pertinent family data in the student record files; flag the file with a red tab.

Ask for written identification from any persons not well known to the school when they request information about a student or wish to remove a student from the school. Train all staff, regular and occasional, not to give out any information about any student without authorization.

If you suspect the child is in immediate danger, or if the noncustodial parent is being disruptive, call the police.

Custody

Unless the court orders otherwise, a spouse who is granted access to a child of the marriage has the right to make inquiries, and to be given information, as to the health, education, and welfare of the child.

Access

Access rights of a parent, regardless of whether or not the child lives with that parent, may be varied or denied only by written separation agreement or court order. When a noncustodial parent requests physical access to a child, provide the access based on the provisions in the separation agreement or court order.

The custodial parent is the primary contact person who makes day-to-day decisions; this is the individual with whom the school will have the most interaction for issues such as attendance, field trips, course selection, etc. Although it is the responsibility of the custodial parent to share educational information with the noncustodial parent, the noncustodial parent should receive from the school such information as report cards, graduation ceremony invitations, and newsletters according to district protocol.

Bullying

Schools need to establish a social climate where physical aggression and bullying are not used to gain popularity, maintain group leadership, or influence others to do what they are told to do.

No one deserves to be bullied.

More information on bullying is available in *What Schools Can Do* at www.bullybeware.com.

Collaboration

Listen to what students, teachers, and parents and guardians have to say about the occurrence of bullying in the school. Find ways to involve the school advisory group, the students, and the community in developing a comprehensive schoolwide antibullying plan. Collaborate with staff (e.g., social workers) to identify district-sponsored antibullying programs. Consult principals in other schools; review programs and strategies in place elsewhere.

Code of Conduct

Review school policies and the school code of conduct. The school policy should include a clear definition of bullying and how the school will respond to incidents. The school code of conduct should state the school's commitment to the prevention of bullying.

Provide training for staff and student leaders, and provide resources for integrating antibullying education into the instructional and coinstructional programs at all grade levels.

Supervision

> Principals must make it clear that bullying is never acceptable.
>
> —*Arresting Violence: A Resource Guide for Schools and Their Communities,* P. N. Ross, p. 44

Recognize the covert nature of bullying and that most bullying happens during recess or in unstructured time. Encourage students to report incidents of bullying and to understand the difference between tattling, reporting, and taking care of oneself and others. Provide increased supervision in areas where bullying tends to occur, and provide alternative play areas and quiet spaces for students who are fearful. Recognize and reward students and staff for positive acts of school citizenship.

See Chapter 3, "Negligence and Liability," for further information regarding supervision of students, and also Chapter 21, "Student Behavior and Discipline in the School."

Response

Encourage communication, foster empathy for others, and insist on accountability for personal behavior. Refer frequently to the school's code of conduct. Consistently enforce school policy in the schoolyard, classrooms, and hallways and in e-mail correspondence; apply consequences for bullies. Train staff in effective classroom management and supervision strategies and support their implementation of the school's antibullying plan. Introduce programs such as peer mediation, a buddy system, and social skills and anger management workshops; teach assertiveness and social skills.

When victims are identified, demonstrate concern, keep records, protect the student from further attacks, inform parents or guardians of both the bully and the victim, and administer consequences to the bully.

Call the police when a student or students are suspected of continued serious coercion and inflicting physical or emotional harm. Refer to your district's police/school protocol.

Implementation and Monitoring

Launch the antibullying plan at an assembly; provide brochures or information on the school's Web site and in newsletters for parents and guardians. Keep a log of bullying incidents to recognize patterns. Address the concerns of a parent or guardian whose child is an alleged bully or victim. Take steps to identify best practices in other schools.

> Bullying is reduced if the principal is committed to addressing bullying.
>
> —Bullying at school: A Canadian perspective,
> A. Charach, D. Pepler, and S. Ziegler, *Education Canada*, 35, p. 12

Suicide Intervention

Train staff and educate students about suicide intervention and prevention. Understand depression and mental health issues that affect youth. Utilize qualified district office staff and teachers to train peer counselors in middle and high schools and create student support groups.

Identify suicide crisis centers, telephone hotlines, support groups, and outreach teams; build awareness about where to turn for help. Link information, help lines, etc., to the school's Web site and highlight resources in the newsletter. Establish connections among the district's student services team, community mental health professionals, and school staff.

Ensure that each student has at least one adult advocate. Promote and support any teacher adviser program. Recommend that parents and guardians maintain open lines of communication with their children.

If there is a suicide at the school, follow your district's response plan. Involve personnel from the district office and other principals to support students, parents, and staff.

Homeless Children and Youth

Barriers to Education

Students without homes are often behind in school because of transience and absenteeism. High school students have great difficulty in completing credits. Students may not make friends, participate in class discussions or coinstructional programs, or bond easily with teachers. Homeless students may come to school hungry and be unable to pay for school supplies, enrichment activities, tickets for social events, transportation, etc.

Homeless children often have little or no involvement with stimulating activities to promote their physical and intellectual growth. Students living in temporary shelters or on the street do not develop study skills or have a place to study. Some students may not have developed age-appropriate life skills and may lack essential health and dental care. During vacation periods, young children may be left alone in unsafe situations.

Immunization records, transcripts, birth certificates, guardianship records, special education information, and the student's records may be hard to track down.

Strategies

1. Foster a school climate that will nurture homeless students and provide for stability, security, belonging, friendship, and adult advocacy. Educate the staff and school advisory group about homelessness and poverty. Seek creative ways to offer before- and after-school programs; weekend, holiday, and summer programs; and tutoring for homeless children. Ensure that children and youth have access to school supplies, a place to store personal belongings, clothes, hygiene products, nutritious meals, a place to study, recreational activities and sports equipment, and transportation.

2. Follow district procedures for enrolling students without permanent addresses and follow protocols for sharing information about transient students and their families. Inquire about district tracking of transient students. If a student must move out of the school's immediate area, attempt to find transportation so the student can continue in the same school, in accordance with district policies. Report to the child protection agency children under the age of 16 who have no apparent parent or guardian or fixed address, or who are runaways.

3. Develop partnerships with local community social agencies and shelters. Provide information to students and parents or guardians regarding community resources and health services. Although it is necessary to protect personal privacy, share information with community social agencies about the needs of homeless children and youth. Through shelters and community support programs, share information about school programs with parents or guardians and caregivers of homeless children and youth.

Many of the above barriers and strategies concerning homeless children and youth are also relevant to children living in poverty or in shelters.

Look After Yourself

You will spend a lot of time looking after others. Be sure to look after yourself too.

Determine your priorities in life: personal health, family, friends, and work.

Learn how to manage stress: read the literature, take a workshop, develop an action plan to deal with stress.

If you have children of your own, give them permission to have a balanced life by modeling that yourself.

The Voice of Experience

24 Occupational Health and Safety

→ GETTING STARTED

Consider how you would handle the following issues:

- A hazardous chemical is seeping into the school's water system.

- The floor in the gymnasium is chipped and cracked.

- Staff who use the portables are complaining of headaches and increased asthma attacks.

- The temperature within the building is above 80 degrees Fahrenheit during warm May and June days.

- The entrances to the school during winter are not cleared of snow and are frequently slippery.

DUTIES OF THE PRINCIPAL

1. Generally legislation stipulates the responsibilities of school districts and the role of principals in administrating and enforcing the legislation. Because the principal may not be the direct supervisor of all staff in the school (e.g., custodians), these responsibilities are shared with other district personnel.

- Review the district's occupational health and safety policy and procedures.

- Review related district policies and procedures; these may cover topics ranging from smoking on district premises to information systems designed to reduce the risk from hazardous products in the workplace.

- Review collective agreements for clauses related to occupational health and safety.

2. Some of the duties may include ensuring that workers do the following:

- Work in the manner and with the protective measures and procedures that the workers' employer requires

- Use or wear the equipment, protective devices, or clothing that the workers' employer requires to be used or worn

- Know of the existence of any potential or actual danger to their health or safety

3. In addition, you have many other related duties, including those listed below.

- Maintaining proper order and discipline in the school

- Giving assiduous attention to the health and comfort of the pupils; to the cleanliness, temperature, and ventilation of the school; to the care of all teaching materials and other school property; to the condition and appearance of the school property; and to the condition and appearance of the school buildings and grounds

- Reporting promptly to the supervisory officer when you have reason to suspect the existence of any communicable disease in the school or of any unsanitary condition on any part of the school buildings or grounds

- Inspecting the school premises at least once a week and reporting forthwith to the district if repairs to the school are, in your opinion, required

- Reporting to the district any lack of attention on the part of the building maintenance staff

- Arranging for at least one emergency drill for emergencies other than those occasioned by fire (Note: These emergency drills must be held during the period in which instruction is given, including evening classes or classes conducted outside the school year.)

CONDUCTING A SCHOOL SAFETY INSPECTION

> The goal of a workplace inspection should be to identify hazards that can lead to injury/illness or property damage.
>
> —Conducting effective workplace inspections:
> Identifying hazards that can lead to injury
> and illness, J. Avery, *The Safe Angle,* 4(1), p. 3

1.   Consult your district's policy about the frequency and types of inspections required. Ensure the appropriate involvement of unions when scheduling and carrying out inspections. Involve the school staff in assisting with inspections and use this as a strategy to raise awareness about safety issues and continuous improvement.

2.   Establish procedures and terms of reference for the school safety inspections. Facilitate training on recognition and identification of hazards.

✓   Prepare a school walk-through checklist to gather specific information in areas such as

- Auditorium

- Classrooms

- Common areas, including the cafeteria, parking lots, hallways, and entrances

- Family studies rooms

- Library and computer laboratories

- Photography darkrooms

- Physical education facilities, including ice rinks and swimming pools

- Playing fields and playgrounds

- Portable classrooms

- Science laboratories

- Technology shops

- Visual arts rooms

Before the inspection, review past reports to identify problem areas.

What to Look for in a Standard Classroom Inspection

Fire Safety

- Are legible fire exit and route signs in appropriate locations?

- Is there a Fire Safety Plan and is the teacher aware of the content and location of the plan?

- Are ceilings or exit doors free of combustible material such as artwork, posters, and paper? As a guideline, no more than 20 percent of the total wall surface (including boards, cupboards, windows, etc.) is to be covered with combustible materials.

- Where there is an exit door, is there a clear path around the classroom furniture? As a rule of thumb, the width of the clear path should be the same as the width of the door(s).

Electrical

- Are electrical safety approval labels on all electrical equipment?

- Are there ground pins on three-wire electrical plugs?

- Are electrical outlets, cover plates, and wall switches secure and undamaged?

- Are extension cords three-wire, in good condition, and used for temporary purposes only?

- Are multiuse cords equipped with power bars?

General

- Do windows open easily and stay open according to their design?

- Do air quality, temperature, and ventilation meet applicable standards? Concerns may be determined by conversation with the teacher in the classroom.

- Are ventilation and heating ducts kept unobstructed by books, paper, etc.?

- Are ceiling tiles in place and unbroken, with no sign of mold formation?

- Are the ceiling, walls, and floor free from water leaks?

- Are floor tiles or carpeting securely fastened to reduce trip hazards?

- Are floors free from hazards that could cause slips, trips, and falls?

- Are audiovisual screens and maps securely suspended using fittings designed for the purpose?

- Are shelves or shelving units firmly anchored to the wall? Storage of all items should follow the following guide: heavy objects on low shelves, light objects on high shelves, and breakable objects such as glass items on low shelves.

- Are step stools or small ladders available for accessing stored items from high shelves?

- Is storage on top of wall-mounted cupboards limited to light-weight objects such as empty boxes?

- Do paper cutters have guards in place and is the torsion spring adjusted to hold the blade up when released?

- Are there first aid stations and trained first aiders available? Do all staff know where the stations are located, and are the trained staff locations identified?

- Is there an asbestos management program, and do all staff know where an asbestos log is kept in the school?

3.   After the inspection, consult with district health and safety personnel and community health agencies for information, advice, and solutions to problems. Report recommendations to the district's plant department staff and your supervisor. Recommendations could include ways to eliminate

hazards, upgrade facilities and equipment to meet legislative standards, improve hygiene practices, and meet ongoing maintenance requirements.

Develop Plans for Foreseeable Contingencies

Be sure to have a plan in place to deal with health and safety situations that may arise. For example, know what you will do if the science, physical education, family studies, or shop teacher (or any other teacher in a higher risk area) is absent.

DEVELOPING OCCUPATIONAL HEALTH AND SAFETY PROCEDURES

1. Consult your district's policies and procedures for direction on how to deal with particular areas of the school. If you do not find the elements listed below in your district's procedures, do consider them when developing your school's health and safety procedures:

- Asbestos

- Art supplies

- Athletic equipment and facilities

- Blackboards and white boards

- Ergonomics

- Fire safety

- First aid kits, eye wash stations, and nonlatex gloves

- Floors, entrances, and walkways

- Food safety and cafeteria services

- Mold and mildew

- New carpeting, painting, or construction

- Pesticides, toxic materials, and other hazardous materials

- Printing and duplicating equipment

- Routine maintenance and cleanliness

- Staff training

- Vehicle safety

- Ventilation, lighting, heating, electrical, and cooling systems

- Washrooms and drinking water

2.   Ensure the staff know who the members of the safety committee are and know how to report concerns or questions. Be constantly vigilant that staff comply with health and safety legislation, district policy, and school procedures. Post signs and health and safety information in the staff room, common areas of the school, and classrooms, as appropriate. Include occupational health and safety issues on the agendas of staff, department head, and school advisory group meetings, and in school newsletters and on the Web site.

For further information, see Chapter 3: "Negligence and Liability."

TIPS

Value Staff

Focusing on staff weakness can be negative and is not helpful in building team spirit. Recognizing individual and group strengths is more rewarding.

You'll catch more flies with honey than with vinegar.

As administrators, we often have agendas that seem very important. Teachers have important agendas too.

The Voice of Experience

Emergency Preparedness

At a Glance

- Getting Started
- Preventive Measures
    Emergency Response Committee
    Emergency Response Plan
    Equipment and Information
    Evacuations and Other Emergency Responses
- Reactive Strategies
    Take Control
    Call for Emergency Assistance
    Communicate, Communicate, Communicate
- Follow-Up and Evaluation

⊕ GETTING STARTED

> . . . it is now the principal's responsibility to plan for the unexpected,
> prepare for the unthinkable, and ensure that everything that can be
> done, is done, in case of an emergency.
>
> —*An Administrative Handbook: A View From the
> Elementary Principal's Desk*, L. J. Stevens, p. 54

Review your district's policy and procedures regarding school safety and emergency preparedness. These may include procedures for fire alarms, bomb threats, violent incidents, armed intruders, and severe weather. Because each school building, location, community, and student body is different, principals need to assess their school's ability to respond to a variety of emergencies; for example, response plans will be different in rural and urban areas.

Review the school's crisis response plan and team. Meet with the team for a briefing.

Study the school crisis response plan. Some questions for your consideration are noted in the two sections below.

1. Staff and Student Preparedness

Will the staff know what to do if the principal is not in the building?

Is there a written emergency plan that includes a fire plan and a communication plan?

Is there a binder or other type of organized information system to provide critical information during an emergency?

Do both regular and occasional staff understand the plan and have assigned duties and training?

Are code words for emergencies such as bomb threats or lockdown situations clearly understood by all staff?

Is there an emergency/crisis response team with each member having clearly defined responsibilities?

Are drills for various emergencies conducted and evaluated regularly?

What is the procedure for reporting staff or student accidents or injuries?

Are safety procedures and behavioral expectations described in the student handbook and are consequences stipulated in the code of conduct?

Is the school advisory group aware of the school's crisis response planning and preparation?

2. Safety Equipment

Is equipment readily available (e.g., flashlights and bullhorns)?

Are first aid kits maintained, distributed throughout the building, and available for field trips?

What type of communication systems are there between classrooms, other areas of the school, and the main office? Does the public announcement system have emergency power backup?

Do the principal, vice-principal, and staff supervisor(s) carry walkie-talkies, beepers, or cell phones when supervising the building or grounds?

How are exterior doors positioned in relation to the school grounds and surrounding community? Are they locked during school hours?

Is there an off-site evacuation location for students and staff? Does the school serve as an evacuation center for another school or community agency?

Are there regular inspections of the building and school grounds to ensure proper maintenance, functionality of mechanical systems, and appropriate storage and disposal of hazardous materials?

PREVENTIVE MEASURES

Emergency Response Committee

Use the district's model to develop the school response protocol. Include school staff, district security personnel, union representatives, members of the school advisory group, and community resource persons in the review of the existing school response procedures. Identify problem areas and recommend response protocols.

Assign specific roles to each member of the Emergency Response Committee; for example, crowd control, equipment coordinator, internal communications, trauma and grief counseling, first aid, and parent support.

Conduct an annual evaluation of the crisis response plan. Update equipment and review staff functions.

Emergency Response Plan

1. **Issues**

   Location of the school in relation to potential community hazards

   Distance from community medical and emergency help

   Size and design of the school building and location of entrances and exits

   Availability of off-site evacuation facilities

   Age and size of the student body

   Availability of district services

2. Types of Emergencies

Accident or fire in the community

Assault or suspected rape

Bomb threat

Building system or mechanical malfunction

Chemical or other hazardous spill

Death of a student or staff member at school or at home

Drug overdose, poisoning, or allergic reaction

Field trip incident

Fire in the school

Intruder or confrontational person

Kidnapping, hostage situation, missing child, or murder

Large group disturbance or gang fight

Severe weather or earthquake

Shooting or use of other weapon

TIPS

Evaluate each crisis individually to determine the appropriate level of response.

3. The Fire Plan

Ensure that the school has an up-to-date fire plan and keep copies in the main office, custodian's office, staff room, and other appropriate areas of the school.

Annually inspect each room or area of the school to make certain that the fire exits and exit routes are clearly marked.

Inspect exit routes and doors frequently to ensure they are unobstructed.

4. Crisis Communication

Follow district policies and procedures on crisis communication.

Review school level communication protocols with staff.

Design a simple communication strategy:

- Identify who needs to be notified.
- Specify plans for getting information out.
- Identify responsibility centers.

Prepare a format for messages delivered by staff via phone and the public announcement system. File samples of the following:

- Letters of condolence
- Information letters to parents
- News releases

File the district media or public relations kit.

Establish contacts with emergency personnel in the community.

Foster a positive relationship with the local media.

Equipment and Information

1. Equipment

Stock emergency kits for the main office and other key areas of the school as required. Kits should include the following:

- Class lists
- Cell phones
- Pagers or walkie-talkies
- Emergency phone numbers
- Flashlights
- Radio with batteries
- Battery operated bullhorn
- Blankets
- Office supplies

Ensure ready access to first aid supplies including nonlatex gloves.

Prepare a binder that contains the following:

- A copy of the response plan and other important information
- A list of first aid qualified staff
- A list of students with special medical or mobility needs
- Phone numbers for bus companies, municipal emergency services, and district security personnel
- Maps of the school indicating special areas, utilities shut-off sites, and hazardous materials
- The official fire plan

Place copies of the binder in the main office, custodian's office, and other key areas of the building.

2. Communication

Establish signals for lockdowns, student and staff medical emergencies, bomb threats, and an all-clear to return to the building.

Have a map of the off-site evacuation location and procedures for transporting students there and taking attendance upon arrival.

Establish protocols with the other schools or community agencies for which your school serves as an evacuation site.

Evacuations and Other Emergency Responses

Assign staff to serve as area wardens or prefects to assist with the supervision of evacuations, to communicate instructions when there is no public address system, and to give the all-clear signal once the building has been cleared.

Conduct fire and emergency drills as required by district policy. Evaluate the results.

Train staff in evacuation procedures; for example, taking the most recent attendance record with them in an evacuation or locking the door when the area is cleared in a lockdown.

Train staff and secondary school students not to go to the parking lot or remove their vehicles in emergencies.

Develop evacuation procedures that include staging areas for students to assemble when they leave the building; involvement of fire, police, health unit, or emergency measures personnel; and provision for disabled or special needs students.

Consider when to use lockdowns to keep students behind locked classroom doors and what to do with students who may be in common areas.

Consult the district's procedures regarding conditions under which you can send students and staff home in an emergency.

REACTIVE STRATEGIES

Take Control

Assess the situation and determine the level and type of response. For example, a hazardous spill may require an immediate evacuation; an armed intruder may require a lockdown; a boiler failure may require calling the buses to take students home.

Activate the portion of the emergency response plan or fire plan appropriate to the situation. Provide immediate first aid. Ensure a safe evacuation staging area and protection from inclement weather. Investigate and search as required.

In the event of a bomb threat, do not touch anything and do not use shortwave radios or cell phones that might activate the bomb.

Call for Emergency Assistance

When you call for assistance, give specific information to the police, ambulance, and firefighters. Do not move any victims; call immediately for help. Cooperate with fire, police, and medical personnel when they arrive.

Inform parents and guardians of student victims and ensure they have transportation to the hospital. When no parent is available to be with a student at the hospital, send a staff member.

TIPS

Give specific information when calling for emergency assistance.

"There are approximately 45 students and nonstudents at the front of the school building. Some have knives and baseball bats and they are threatening to assault each other."

"The student is an 11-year-old girl who has recently been diagnosed as a diabetic. She is currently unconscious and her pulse is weak and thready. Her father has been called. He is five minutes away from the school. What is your estimated time of arrival?"

Communicate, Communicate, Communicate

1. Call your supervisor.

2. Let district personnel communicate with the school district.

3. Keep notes about calls, responses, and procedures. Document, document, document.

4. Get assistance from the district's communication officer. Draft verbal and print statements or news releases that give a brief outline of the incident and indicate how updates can be obtained.

5. Do not release names of students and staff involved in the incident until parents and family have been notified.

6. Share information with parents, students, the school advisory group, supervisor, neighboring schools, community agencies that are housed in the school building, etc., as directed by the district's communication officer.

7. Get all the bad news out at once; then talk only about the actions the school is taking.

8. Provide interviews with the media relaying your three key messages. You may wish to provide interviews through the district's communications officer. If you do not have a district communications officer to assist you with preparations for interviews or press conferences, call the senior communications consultant at your professional association.

9. Do not place blame; state the facts and talk about the solution.

10. Understand what the principal is responsible for; do not speak on behalf of the police, health unit, or anyone else.

If the incident occurs on the weekend or during a holiday, it may be necessary to open the school for use by staff, parents, and students.

See Chapter 6, "Public and Media Relations," for further information on dealing with the media and conducting interviews.

FOLLOW-UP AND EVALUATION

1. All-Clear

Ensure the building is safe for the return of staff and students after an evacuation. Provide for alternative teaching space if a portion of the building is under repair after fire, vandalism, flooding, etc. If the school has been seriously damaged or destroyed, seek assistance from your supervisor, district staff, and community organizations to find temporary space and learning materials.

2. Debriefing

Assemble the school's emergency response team and review their actions. Seek their advice and suggestions. Meet with all staff and brief them. Seek the assistance of the district's tragic events team and staff from other schools.

3. Communication

Prepare a statement for staff members to use when answering phone inquires. Meet with students in small groups to provide follow-up information and answer questions. In some instances, an assembly may be appropriate. Follow district procedures for the reporting of student accidents and staff accidents. With the guidance of the district information officer, prepare a letter for parents, trustees, the media, etc., to offer additional information about the incident and what students can expect.

4. In Case of Death

Generally, districts will have developed a process for all schools. Follow district protocol for lowering the school's flag if there has been a death. Call the family of the victim(s); indicate your concern and offer the support services of the district. Open a book of condolence in the main office or other suitable location. Determine whether the school will hold a memorial service for the deceased and help students and staff with the planning. Close student or staff records according to district procedures. Deal with the victim's personal effects.

Provide rooms where students can meet with peer and staff counselors. Consult with the emergency/crisis response team about how staff and students are coping during the aftermath; identify issues and concerns. Student suicide will require special steps to minimize the possibility that other students may imitate the behavior. Seek guidance from relevant personnel.

Arrange for class coverage for staff who wish to attend the funeral.

Training Opportunities

Take advantage of all training offered by your district in the area of emergency preparedness.

Control Your Reactions and Take Responsibility

Always remember that your response sets the tone for everyone else's.

You may not be able to control circumstances, but you can control the way you react to them.

When you make a mistake (and that will happen), take full responsibility and apologize.

The Voice of Experience

26 Student Medical Needs

At a Glance

- Getting Started
  District Policies and Procedures and School Practices
  Individual Student Needs
  Prevention Programs
- Responding to Specific Situations
  Anaphylaxis: Allergies and Emergency Medical Treatment
  Administration of Medication to Students
  Accidents and Injuries
- Other Health Issues
  Chronic Illness
  Smoking
  Immunization
  Communicable and Infectious Diseases
- A Comprehensive School Health Program
  Social, Medical, and Physical Support
  Preventive Health

→ GETTING STARTED

District Policies and Procedures and School Practices

Follow district policies and procedures regarding student health issues. These policies might include the following topics:

- Administration of medication to students

- Anaphylaxis

- Communicable diseases

- First aid and training

- HIV/AIDS

- Reporting an accident or injury

Review district policies, procedures, and expectations with regular and occasional staff. Educate staff about the duty of teachers, principals, and vice-principals to accommodate the needs of students with chronic illnesses or conditions or life-threatening allergies. Ask the vice-principal or office coordinator to brief you concerning school practices for administering medication to students, responding to injured students, and managing students with anaphylaxis, asthma, diabetes, epilepsy, etc.

Think in terms of both preventive and reactive strategies. Consider what needs to be done before, during, and after an injury or accident, an anaphylactic reaction, the administration of medication to students, etc.

Ensure that these school practices follow district policies and procedures.

For further information regarding standard of care, see Chapter 3: "Negligence and Liability."

Individual Student Needs

Identify students with chronic illnesses or conditions or life-threatening allergies. Determine students' circumstances and needs. Meet individually with them and/or their parents.

Collect information regarding the medical needs of all new students. Update medical information annually for returning students, including district-specific administration of medication forms. Ensure that medical information concerning individual students is communicated to all staff who need to know. Request a physician-prescribed action plan for each student requiring support to attend school.

See "Responding to Specific Situations" below for further details regarding the following:

- Anaphylaxis: emergency medical treatment and allergies

- Administration of medication to students

- Accidents and injuries

Prevention Programs

Communicate regularly to all parents and students the steps being taken at the school to reduce health risks for pupils. Ensure that individual students with health issues are not identified. Be prepared to address the attitudes and concerns that some staff, students, and parents may have regarding any new prevention protocols being implemented at the school.

Involve the staff and school advisory group in the planning of prevention and intervention programs. Determine what outside resources are available to assist with prevention programming. Develop prevention programs in partnership with community agencies and the health department. Implement appropriate prevention programs (e.g., peanut-free programs designed to reduce health risks). Evaluate the school's prevention programs regularly.

Reduce the risk for students with life-threatening allergies and chronic conditions through careful planning that takes into account such factors as cafeteria services and menus, accommodations for eating lunch, risks on field trips, school painting and maintenance protocols, and the use of nontoxic cleaning materials and pesticides.

Arrange for training of staff where appropriate (e.g., Heimlich maneuver, administration of epinephrine).

RESPONDING TO SPECIFIC SITUATIONS

Anaphylaxis: Allergies and Emergency Medical Treatment

1. Check all collective agreements regarding the administration of epinephrine and student medication by staff. Review the district's policies and procedures regarding emergency medical treatment and allergies. Ensure that the school plan for dealing with anaphylaxis follows district procedures and outlines both preventive and reactive strategies.

2. Insist that parents of anaphylactic students provide a current assessment of their children's condition and a physician-prescribed plan. Train staff to handle anaphylactic emergencies (e.g., in the use of epinephrine). Keep epinephrine close to students; older students may carry their own epinephrine for easy access.

3. When developing or revising your school's anaphylaxis plan, consider the elements noted in the six areas below.

    a. Ways to encourage parents of an anaphylactic student to identify the student

       What the school is prepared to do to support an anaphylactic student

       A process to inform all students, staff, and parents of their responsibilities

       A communications plan that outlines the district's policy

    b. A procedure for publishing specific medical details regarding individual students for the information of all staff

       A written emergency protocol form for each student with anaphylaxis, and a signed permission form for the emergency use of epinephrine

    c. An emergency response plan that includes transporting the student to a hospital

       A plan to deal with anaphylaxis occurring on the school bus, in lunchroom facilities, at social events where food is served, on field trips, at special seasonal activities, etc.

       Annual training of regular staff, occasional staff, older students, and volunteers in the use of epinephrine.

    d. Methods to minimize and control allergens such as those found in insect bites, nuts, commercially prepared foods and candy, art supplies, toys, mold, paint, and carpets.

    e. A buddy system for students

       A procedure for responding to teasing or bullying of anaphylactic students

    f. An annual review of the school's preventive and reactive procedures regarding anaphylaxis

Information About Anaphylaxis

A highly recommended resource is available online at www.cdnsba.org.

Administration of Medication to Students

1. Follow your district's policies and procedures regarding the administration of medication to students. Check all collective agreements (teachers, educational assistants, office staff) for any clauses concerning the administration of medication by staff.

2. When reviewing your school protocol for administering medication, consider the elements noted in the five areas below:

   a. The availability of qualified staff, the provision of staff training, and the creation of an updated list of designated staff

   The degree to which administering medication interferes with other regular duties of staff

   b. The district-required authorization form signed by the parent, with instructions from a physician, updated each September

   The possible side effects involved in administering the medication

   c. The number of students requiring medication regularly or on an as-needed basis

   The various types of medication provided and their storage requirements (e.g., refrigeration)

   Labeling of all medications and photo of student

   d. Medication storage

   A protocol for checking the age of medication

   A location for safe, secure, and accessible storage of medications

   e. Medication administration

   A private location for administering or supervising the administration of medication

   The use of log sheets to record details regarding the administration of medication, including pupil's name, date, time of administration, dosage given, and name of person administering.

A response plan for dealing with emergencies arising from the administering of medication

Locations for first aid kits (e.g., in the office, gymnasium, cafeteria, science laboratories, on field trips)

Procedures for administering medication or emergency treatment when students are off-site

Further Reading Regarding Managing Medication

Chapter 8, "Managing Medication in the Schools," in *An Educator's Guide to the Role of the Principal*, by E. M. Roher and S. Wormwell, covers duty and standard of care in ordinary circumstances and in an emergency, assignment to administer medication, managing students with diabetes, and managing students with allergies.

Accidents and Injuries

Follow your district's policies and procedures when responding to and reporting student accidents and injuries. When developing the school plan for responding to accidents and injuries, consider what will happen before (accident prevention), during (reaction and response), and after (follow-up) an injury.

1. Before

    a. Planning

    Check all collective agreements for any clauses concerning the administration of first aid by staff.

    Review and comply with relevant safety legislation and district policies and procedures regarding school facilities, instructional activities, and coinstructional activities.

    Review the school's overall emergency response plan.

    Develop reporting and communication protocols in case of a serious accident.

    Develop and regularly review a crisis communication plan.

    b. Training

    Identify which staff members have first aid training, training in the use of automated electronic defibrillators (AEDs), and CPR training.

Provide first aid training opportunities for staff, especially those working in the office and gym.

Train staff and students in the safe use of equipment and supplies, ranging from glue guns to chemicals in the science laboratories.

Provide training for staff on how to respond to an accident or injury.

c. Prevention

Communicate general accident and injury prevention strategies to staff, students, parents, volunteers, and the school advisory group; motivate participation in accident prevention activities.

Display first aid and accident prevention posters and information in the staff room, main office, classrooms, and common areas of the school.

Review specific accident prevention and reaction programs in science laboratories, industrial arts and family studies rooms, physical education programs, school buses, and other critical areas.

d. Risk assessment

Practice general risk assessment and safety planning strategies; for example, conduct a site safety audit.

Identify specific hazards or temporary hazards in the school or on school grounds.

Identify students with special health needs or disabilities.

For further information, see Chapter 24, "Occupational Health and Safety," and Chapter 25, "Emergency Preparedness."

e. First aid kits

Ensure that first aid kits containing updated supplies are located throughout the building and provided on field trips.

Inform staff, students, substitute teachers, and volunteers about the location of first aid kits and trained first aid personnel.

Inform staff, students, substitute teachers, and volunteers of the procedures for responding to and reporting accidents.

Ensure staff compliance with procedures to prevent infection when dealing with bodily fluids (e.g., the use of disposable gloves).

2. When an Injury Occurs

a. Report the injury to the office.

b. Make sure someone stays with the student.

    c. Administer first aid if needed; call for a trained first aider from the list maintained at the school.

    d. Arrange for medical assistance and transportation by ambulance to the hospital, if necessary.

    e. Have a staff member go to the hospital with the student and take printed information concerning the student.

    f. Inform the student's parents or guardians.

    g. Be sure to complete and submit an accident report in a timely fashion, following district procedures. This is a critical step to take when an injury occurs.

    h. Use your district's accident report forms and maintain a log regarding accidents.

    i. Inform your supervisor and district personnel immediately if the injury is serious.

3. After an Injury

    a. Demonstrate concern for the student.

    b. Provide support for staff and students affected by the accident.

    c. Document all details regarding the accident. Be mindful of issues of negligence and liability. See Chapter 3, "Negligence and Liability," for further details.

    d. Consult with your supervisor in the case of a serious accident or injury.

    e. Cooperate with district personnel and their designated insurance agent and legal counsel.

    f. Do not discuss the situation with agents appointed by the student's family; consult your district staff.

    g. Follow your crisis communications plan if the media become involved.

    h. Call your professional association if you would like additional advice and assistance.

TIPS

Note: A principal is required to give assiduous attention to the health and comfort of *all* pupils.

OTHER HEALTH ISSUES

Chronic Illness

Within the context of district policy and physician-directed plans, develop proactive and reactive school procedures and classroom strategies to help staff and students address chronic illnesses and conditions such as asthma, diabetes, epilepsy, cancer, cystic fibrosis, juvenile rheumatoid arthritis, hemophilia, mental illness, HIV/AIDS, and muscular dystrophy. Staff must have an understanding of the medical condition and skills in emergency management that are specific to the individual student. School procedures regarding emergency management of asthma, diabetes, and epilepsy would parallel those for the emergency management of anaphylaxis. In all cases, follow district policy.

Acquaint yourself with district policies and procedures regarding home instruction and other accommodations for long-term illness. Find out what supports are available through district office staff (e.g., social workers and psychologists) and outside agencies to assist chronically ill students and their parents.

Ensure that students with restricted mobility are considered in the development of evacuation plans.

Smoking

In compliance with community bylaws and district policies, students, staff, and members of the community are not permitted to smoke in the school or on school grounds. Stipulate district-approved consequences in the school's code of conduct for possession and use of tobacco products. Support and promote antismoking programs at the school.

Immunization

Parents and guardians are directly responsible for immunization of their children. This law applies to all students under the age of 18 years. The principal may be required to suspend or exclude from school a student who is not immunized as required by the legislation and who is not legally exempt from being immunized. Parents have a right to a hearing before the school board to respond. Follow district procedures for verification of immunization upon registration of students.

Communicable and Infectious Diseases

Follow the established protocol for informing the local public health unit about suspected cases of reportable diseases. Control programs may include tuberculosis, meningitis, chicken pox, influenza, hepatitis B, and HIV/AIDS.

Review health department documentation regarding symptoms, treatment, and exclusions from school associated with various diseases. Review district policy about attendance at school of students with communicable diseases.

Call the public health unit if you have specific questions regarding infectious diseases. The health unit will consult with and provide information to staff, parents, and students about communicable disease concerns and issues.

Pediculosis

Pediculosis is not considered to be a disease. It is, however, an issue you may have to deal with at the school.

Review district and health unit protocols and fact sheets regarding head lice.

Use district forms, letters, and information sheets when communicating with parents.

Train volunteers to conduct screening. Health units do not check heads.

Send general information to all parents and specific information to parents of affected students.

A COMPREHENSIVE SCHOOL HEALTH PROGRAM

While we expect our schools to be places of learning, the role we expect them to play in health is not as clearly defined.

If our schools could promote health as they do learning, holistically and with measures available, the benefits both today and to future generations would be very significant—both in terms of health and education.

—*A National Framework for Health Promoting Schools (2000–2003)*

When developing a comprehensive school health plan, follow your district's policies and procedures, the curriculum guidelines, and various special education requirements. As you develop your plan, consider (among others) the factors listed below.

Social, Medical, and Physical Support

Counseling, psychological, and social services provided by the district and others

Referrals to, and partnerships with, community agencies

Trauma and grief counseling

Peer counselors, peer helpers, and peer support groups

Mentoring

Teacher adviser programs

Stress management programs for staff and students

Staff wellness programs

Health screening and fitness testing and promotion

Healthy role models

Modifications to the school building and classrooms for wheelchairs.

Preventive Health

1. Review the preventive health programs currently offered through the district, which might include the following:

   a. Safe driving and impaired driving

   b. Smoking cessation

   c. Substance abuse

   d. Suicide

   e. Eating disorders

   f. Head lice

   g. Sun protection and skin cancer

   h. Sexually transmitted diseases and hepatitis

   i. Sexual abstinence

   j. Date rape

   Several of the above intervention programs are culturally sensitive and require careful handling.

2. Review the services currently offered at the school that contribute to a comprehensive school health program:

    a. Services related to speech, hearing, and sight

    b. Dental and oral health services

    c. Nutrition, weight management, and cafeteria services

    d. Mental health and depression services

    e. School-based health centers (treatment and rehabilitation)

    f. After-school programs

    g. Preschool and school readiness programs

    h. School and community social workers and psychologists

    i. Health unit

    j. Physicians

    k. Police

    l. Fire department

Further Reading Regarding Student Health

Anderson, A. (Ed.) (2001) Healthy Schools/Healthy Kids, special issue of *Orbit*.

Greene, L. E. (Ed.) (2002) Children's Heath & Safety, special issue of *Principal*.

Call On Colleagues; Build a Network

Talk with colleagues. They are a source and a resource.

Just knowing that there is someone out there who can help is a great comfort.

Gather wisdom from those who have more experience than you do.

The Voice of Experience

PART V

Looking
After Yourself

27

Professional Learning and Personal Well-Being

At a Glance

- An Overview: Professional Learning
    School Administration Team
    Professional Portfolios
    Conferences
    Workshops and Training Sessions
    Mentors
    Networking
    Personal Code of Conduct
- Professional Reading
- Personal Well-Being
    Stress Management: A Questionnaire
    Ten Suggestions for Reducing Stress
    Know Where to Get Help

⊙ AN OVERVIEW: PROFESSIONAL LEARNING

Be sure to continue with your professional development activities now that you are a principal. Although you are very busy, you still need to make time for your professional learning. It's good for your personal well-being, and it's important to model lifelong learning for students and staff.

Remember, you cannot be an expert in everything all at once. Set a focus for yourself and establish your priorities over a three- to five-year cycle.

School Administration Team

Build a positive working relationship with your vice-principal, if you have one. Meet regularly to discuss day-to-day operations. Be sure to build in time for mutual professional growth; discuss research trends, instructional strategies, or leadership literature. Learn from each other's strengths; share constructive feedback. The vice-principal is the only individual in the school with whom you can share certain information and discuss particular situations. Building a supportive professional relationship will reduce the isolation and provide an ongoing opportunity for meaningful professional growth.

Professional Portfolios

> Those who do not reflect lose sight of the fact that their everyday reality is only one of many possible alternatives. They tend to forget the purposes and ends toward which they are working.
> —*Preparing for Reflective Teaching*,
> C. A. Grant and K. M. Zeichner

Although the role of administrator is demanding and offers a considerable number of varied learning opportunities, it is still important to keep a focused perspective on personal professional growth. One of the best ways of achieving this perspective is to maintain a professional portfolio.

There are essentially three major types of professional portfolios, each of which, although different in structure, intent, and audience, offers important opportunities for self-reflection and the determination of future personal professional development activities. In preparing these portfolios the administrator takes the time to reflect upon accomplishments, growth, competencies, and needs and puts current and future actions into a clearer perspective.

Personal Growth Portfolios

- Are the most loosely structured and comprehensive of the three types

- Are designed to suit the needs of the individual

- Provide opportunities for self-reflection and personal planning

- Are designed to outline statements of philosophy, to record experiences, to demonstrate competencies and accomplishments, and to set future goals and courses of action

- Are intended for use by the author who also may choose to share them with trusted colleagues or cognitive coaches

Evaluation Portfolios

- Are kept to identify statements of philosophy and goals and to document those events, experiences, and competencies that are stressed by the employer in order to demonstrate proficiency in the position

- Are structured to reflect the guidelines or expectations articulated by the employer

- Are used during periods of assessment to demonstrate competence and excellence

- Are intended for use by the evaluator

Promotion Portfolios

- Are developed to demonstrate relevant personal philosophies, proficiency, and preparedness for a specific desired position

- Are semistructured in that they are organized to reflect the values and requisite competencies of the organization and the position desired; yet there is some personal latitude in the way in which they are designed

- Are intended for use by the prospective employer

As varied as these types of portfolios may be, there is still some content that is common to all. Portfolios usually contain the following common components in one form or another:

- A table of contents

- A statement of philosophy and goals

- A current résumé

- Artifacts (materials produced during normal completion of the job)

- Productions (materials produced for the purpose of the portfolio)

- Narratives (explanations of significance for each artifact and production)

- Attestations and accolades

- Professional development records

- Community involvement records

The maintenance of a professional portfolio is an individual, fluid activity involving many personal choices regarding structure, format, and content. This activity provides very important opportunities for self-reflection, setting goals, recording accomplishments and accolades, outlining a history of growth, demonstrating competencies, outlining future courses of action, and clarifying your purpose, philosophy, and practice. A professional portfolio demonstrates where you have been, the current context of your position, and a focus and direction for the future.

Further Reading

Brown, G., and Irby, B. J. (1997) *The Principal Portfolio.*

Conferences

Keep up-to-date on conferences being offered. Don't assume that you cannot go due to funding or time constraints. If you find a conference that meets your needs and fits in with your professional goals, ask colleagues and your supervisor how you can make it happen.

Workshops and Training Sessions

Take part in professional development and other practical training opportunities offered by your district for new school administrators.

Mentors

Identify an experienced principal in the district who is willing to act as your mentor. This may be an individual mentor, or it may be a cohort mentor who is working with a small group of new administrators. If the district has a formal mentoring program, take part in it.

Discuss with your mentor mutual goals for the mentoring relationship, a meeting schedule, strategies for communication between meetings, your particular issues of concern (e.g., budget), records to be kept (e.g., a professional journal), and other questions. Build in a review process.

Networking

Attend superintendent or area meetings for principals and vice-principals, district workshops and training sessions, and local professional meetings.

Form a support group that includes new and experienced colleagues, or form a support group composed solely of new principals; these are sometimes referred to as *co-mentoring* groups. Have breakfast or lunch with colleagues. Informal networking is invaluable; don't skip it. Form electronic networking groups.

Create work groups to complete tasks collaboratively, especially for those jobs that all principals share (e.g., school profiles). These are sometimes referred to as Worksmart or Round Table sessions, where common assignments can be completed with colleagues and an expert local coach, combining professional development and task completion.

At the very least, develop a personal roster of local experts to call, prior to finalizing important decisions, especially if you are a sole administrator.

Personal Code of Conduct

Develop your own personal code of conduct. Review and revise it from time to time. The sample below is from *The New Manager's Starter Kit:*

Maintain absolute integrity in all things at all times.

Praise in public; criticize in private.

Treat your word as bond; keep your promises.

Always be on time.

Accept responsibility for your actions.

SOURCE: Adapted from *The New Manager's Starter Kit*, R. Crittendon, p. 16.

📖 PROFESSIONAL READING

Look for professional articles and books that give practical advice to new school leaders. Set priorities; you can't do everything all at once. Give yourself credit for the aspects of your work that you already have under control. The list below gives titles of some recommended works and outlines their contents.

Getting Through Year One by Joan Daly-Lewis

1. The staff

   If it works, don't fix it.

   Fight the jump reflex.

   Let go; delegate.

2. The work

   Get to know the culture of your school and district.

   View the year in terms of functional seasons.

   Leave footprints.

3. Personal survival

   Seek a mentor, confidant, and advisor.

   Identify and consult with the building's informational leaders.

   Don't take yourself or others too seriously.

A Letter to Newly Appointed Principals: Ten Tips for Making the Grade by Kevin Skelly

1. Understand the power of the position.

2. Have a mentor.

3. Listen.

4. Be humble.

5. Do something safe, dramatic, and visible early.

6. Find out as much as possible about your predecessors and where the land mines are.

7. Ask people for advice on how to make decisions, and move slowly to change existing policies.

8. Be an educational leader.

9. Be positive.

10. Keep things in perspective.

**"Starting on the Right Foot: A Blueprint for Incoming Principals"
by Lawrence Roder and David Pearlman**

1. Designing an entry plan

2. Finding out what matters: get to know the school and community

3. The job versus the job description

***Ten Principles for New Principals: A Guide to Positive Action* by
Mark Joel**

1. Change is constant.

2. A principalship is a power position.

3. First impressions are lasting impressions.

4. All things are not created equal.

5. Allow other lights to shine.

6. People share their interpretation of your message.

7. The buck stops here.

8. Together is better.

9. Accountability counts.

10. Work smarter.

***The 7 Habits of Highly Effective People* by Stephen Covey**

1. Be proactive.

2. Begin with the end in mind.

3. Put first things first.

4. Think win-win.

5. Seek first to understand, then to be understood.

6. Synergize.

7. Sharpen the saw.

***What Makes a Leader?* by Daniel Goleman**

The five components of emotional intelligence at work

1. Self-awareness

2. Self-regulation

3. Motivation

4. Empathy

5. Social skill

PERSONAL WELL-BEING

✅ Stress Management: A Questionnaire

You have a very demanding job. Be sure to monitor your workload and behavior and the impact they are having on your body. Start by answering the following questions:

☐ Do you get a knot in your stomach, headaches, or other physiological sensations at work or while thinking about work?

☐ Does your heart race on Sunday night thinking about work and what you have to do tomorrow?

☐ Are you missing out on social, family, or personal occasions because of work?

☐ Do you put off medical and dental appointments because you are too busy?

☐ Does time off, such as vacations, cause more stress than working?

☐ When you are off, do you have difficulty leaving the work behind?

☐ Do you feel like a martyr as you tell others how much overtime you have put in?

☐ Does being at work make you feel better than being anywhere else?

☐ Do you feel pressure from colleagues or superiors to work longer and later because they do?

☐ Do you have the expectation that others should keep the pace and hours you choose to keep?

SOURCE: Adapted from Do You Stop to Smell the Roses? L. Beresford, *The Register*, 3(4), pp. 30–33.

Depending on your responses to these questions, you may want to take a closer look at your priorities. Perhaps you would benefit from trying to put some balance back into your life or from practicing some stress management techniques as described below.

TIPS Ten Suggestions for Reducing Stress

1. Allow time for relaxation, hobbies, sports, TV, vacations.

2. Rest is essential. Have a nap; go to bed early.

3. Regular meals are essential as well. Don't skip lunch.

4. Start to work out; you'll decrease stress.

5. Humor does wonders. Lighten up at home and at school.

6. What you model sets a tone that can contribute to the guilt that other staff members may feel. Do not reward overwork.

7. Keep your hours at school, and at home, reasonable.

8. Do not feel guilty when you leave work early (which for most people is really on time) to attend meaningful events in your personal life.

9. Don't allow your work alone to define you.

10. Define yourself by your ability to balance work-related stress.

SOURCE: Do You Stop to Smell the Roses? L. Beresford, *The Register*, 3(4), pp. 30–33.

Note: No amount of reading will, by itself, reduce your stress or add balance to your life. Picking just one item from the above list, and changing your behavior in that one area, will make a difference.

> **Personal resiliency is a key
> to a successful career in administration.**
>
> Principals need to accept that change is ongoing, that they alone are responsible for their attitudes, that they have control of their lives, that their ongoing learning is important to working smarter, and that they need to take time to reflect on their successes.
>
> —*Ten Principles for New Principals:
> A Guide to Positive Action*, M. Joel, p. 63

Know Where to Get Help

If you are dealing with excessive stress, know where to get assistance:

- Your professional association for professional advice and assistance

- The district's Employee Assistance Program (EAP)

- Your family doctor

Look After Yourself

Maintaining balance between your personal and professional life is essential. Not only is it healthy for you as an individual, but it also sends a positive message to your staff.

Be fit. Begin a physical fitness program and eat properly.

Take time for yourself to relax and re-energize.

The Voice of Experience

28 Support for School Leaders

WHAT TO DO WHEN YOU NEED HELP

When you are dealing with a difficult situation or a crisis, it's essential to consult others. Discuss the matter with the following people:

1. Vice-principal

2. Supervisor

3. Professional association

4. Mentor

5. Colleagues

6. Other experts at your district

7. District's lawyer

8. Other professionals, as appropriate

When you are dealing with a particularly difficult situation, call your professional association for advice, assistance, and support.

WHEN TO CALL YOUR PROFESSIONAL ASSOCIATION FOR ASSISTANCE

 Be sure to call your professional association and ask to speak with a senior staff consultant when

- you are served with a subpoena or a statement of claim,

- you are dealing with a difficult parent,

- a complaint has been filed against you,

- you are called as a witness,

- you are contemplating staff discipline,

- there are complaints or accusations against you from union members,

- you are having difficulty with your supervisor or vice-principal,

- principals or vice-principals in your district are having difficulty with senior administration,

- you are facing discipline from your district,

- questions arise about long-term disability, pension and retirement, leaves of absence, or transfer to another district.

When there's been a serious accident, or you are dealing with a school crisis, or there is significant media involvement, take all the appropriate first steps according to district procedures.

Call On Colleagues; Build a Network

Asking someone's advice is a sincere form of flattery.

Build a support network.

Attend any professional association workshops that you can; they provide valuable and useful information on how to do the job.

The Voice of Experience

Appendices and Resources

Appendix A

Entry Plans

Design your own entry plan when you are appointed to a new school. You will find suggestions for your entry plan in the four sections below.

THE OBJECTIVES

Your entry plan may seek

- a smooth transition of the school administration,

- to build positive relationships,

- to gain information about the school organization,

- to become familiar with the physical plant,

- to understand the core values of the school.

THE PROCESS

The process will likely include

- identifying internal and external groups,

- collecting information from these groups,

- meeting with key individuals,

- sharing the results of your inquiries,

- setting your initial directions and goals.

Patience Is a Virtue

The hardest battle you will have to fight in the entry process is your own desire to change the world.

—Starting on the right foot: A blueprint
for incoming principals, L. Roder and
D. Pearlman, *NASSP Bulletin, 73*(519), p. 75

THE ACTIVITIES

Meet with

- the superintendent of schools about school directions;
- your local board of education, if appropriate;
- the outgoing principal;
- the vice-principal, if there is one;
- the staff (teaching and nonteaching);
- the chair of the school advisory group;
- the chair of the student council.

Take a tour of the school and grounds; observe the condition of the buildings and yard.

Find out what special programs are offered at the school; arrange to see them in action.

Drive around the community to get a sense of its characteristics.

Meet with community partners, cultural leaders, etc.

An essential component to improving your school and student learning is to have the stakeholders trust you as a leader.

First impressions are important; therefore, developing an effective entry plan that will recognize the needs of the school, develop the relationships necessary to ensure change, and promote your vision as a leader are all vital.

—Entry plan: More than just a checklist, by J. Atherton,
The Register, 4(1), pp. 29–31

THE INQUIRIES

The key question is: *What do I want to know about my new school?* When developing your entry plan, ask yourself what you want to know about each aspect of the school. As you conduct your entry plan meetings and tours, inquire about the status of the following items:

1. School profile

    School Web site

    School newsletters

    School calendar

    Student yearbook and newspaper

    Student, parent, and staff handbooks

    School policies (e.g., homework)

2. School advisory groups

    School advisory group minutes and annual report

    PTA or Home and School Association

3. The school community

    Equity, diversity, and inclusion issues

    Special school or community groups

    Before- and after-school programs

    Community use of the school

    Volunteers in the school

    Local board of education

    Superintendent or director(s)

4. Status of staffing and vacancies

    Teaching assignments

    Educational assistants

    Office assistants

    Custodians

    Unions in the school, union stewards, and collective agreements

5. Staff supervision and evaluation process at the school

    Absence reporting

    Occasional and emergency teachers

    Staff development plan

Beginning teacher induction program

Staff recognition and awards programs

6. School organization

Timetables

Supervision and duty schedules (including inclement weather)

Leadership structures

Team, division, grade, and department structure and minutes of meetings

Staff meetings and minutes

Staff social and recreational events

7. Routines for the first day of school

Daily routines for entry, dismissal, etc.

Schoolyard and boundaries

Lunch arrangements

Morning announcements (PA)

Transportation arrangements

8. Administration of student medication

Safe schools issues particular to the site

Emergency plans (e.g., fire, bomb, intrusion, weather, early closing)

Crisis response team

Medical personnel (i.e., nurse, if available)

9. Student behavior and discipline

School code of conduct

Dress code

10. Feeder schools

Destinations of graduates

Statistics regarding student attendance, graduation, dropouts, suspension, expulsion, etc.

11. School improvement plan

Other school plans

Standardized test results

12. Instructional programs

    Special education program, tracking of referrals, IEPs

    Literacy

    Numeracy

    Communication and information technology

13. Coinstructional program

    Special events and assemblies

    Student council and student leadership activities

    Special programs (e.g., breakfast programs, before- and after-school programs)

    Awards program

14. School budget (surplus/deficit)

    School budget accounts

    Accounting practices (software)

    Cash advance

    Credit cards

    Banking

    Nondistrict (nonpublic) funds

    Fundraising

    Purchasing program

    School supplies

15. School plant: maintenance and repairs

    Keys, security codes and telephone numbers, alarms, clocks, bells

16. Current hot spots

Appendix B

Principals' Routines

A SAMPLE SCHOOL PRINCIPAL'S ROUTINES

Daily Routines

1. Assess building readiness. Check in with custodians.

2. Assess staff readiness (i.e., need for substitute class coverage).

3. Greet the students each morning in the front foyer. Be in the halls during class changes.

4. Eat lunch with the students in the cafeteria on occasion. Eat lunch with staff on occasion.

5. Be in the front foyer as the students leave in the afternoon.

6. Make the announcements each day, pointing out the most recent accomplishments of staff and students.

7. Circle through the staff room at noon hour and before school to offer friendly greetings.

8. Walk through the entire school at least once in the morning and once in the afternoon.

9. Make a point of greeting everyone with a smile.

10. Never walk by a situation where students are not carrying out school policy.

11. Drop into one or two classes during daily rounds for a friendly interaction with students.

12. Report to the maintenance staff any areas that need cleaning or repair.

13. Meet with the student leaders.

14. Clear all mail and correspondence off your desk.

Weekly Routines

1. Meet with the administrative team to go over calendars and be briefed on each area of responsibility.

2. Review progress on academic initiatives.

3. Monitor activity in staffing and school program portfolio.

4. Review plant projects to see that they are on track.

5. Attend at least one student activity after school.

6. Attend all semifinal and final games of school teams.

7. Consciously think to praise staff and students for particular things they have done.

Monthly Routines

1. Meet with department heads to review responsibilities and initiatives.

2. Meet with staff to review responsibilities and provide professional development. (Check collective agreement.)

3. Meet with the chair of the school advisory group.

4. Attend the school advisory group meeting.

5. Chair the school academic initiatives committee meeting.

6. Attend school social activities.

7. Visit classes for teacher performance appraisals.

8. Attend principals' association meeting.

9. Attend district superintendency meeting.

10. Attend district school reform committee meetings.

11. Attend program review committee meetings.

12. Review budget expenditures with staff.

13. Attend in-school committee meetings as often as possible.

14. Maintain a positive attitude toward change in all staff meetings and informal interactions with staff.

15. Review the environment of the school to ensure that academics have priority.

16. Reinforce at every staff gathering that students must be treated fairly and be given due process in every situation.

Quarterly Routines

1. Review all class data; compute the school average.

2. Review program procedures such as districtwide testing.

3. Meet with parents of students involved in cultural exchanges.

4. Review Information and Communication Technology Plan.

5. Attend at least one professional development activity.

6. Contribute to the school newsletter.

7. Review all student report cards.

8. Attend school dances.

9. Monitor commencement activities.

10. Follow through on initiatives; for example, the administration team might check Grade 9 notebooks on a random sampling basis.

Yearly Routines

1. Review and edit the teacher handbook.

2. Review and edit safe-schools procedures.

3. Submit teacher performance appraisals for designated staff.

4. Plan initiatives for enrichment programs.

5. Run in-service for all new staff and all staff in general.

6. Hire new staff.

7. Update the staff phone tree for emergencies.

8. Plan a celebration for those leaving the staff.

9. Submit the plan for school plant improvements.

10. Set the budget with departments.

11. Establish supervision schedules with the administrative team.

12. Establish a timetable for the year with the administrative team.

13. Visit a student leadership camp.

14. Accompany students on at least one field trip.

15. Review the year and plan next year with department heads and vice-principals.

16. Chair the commencement committee.

17. Attend the graduation dance.

18. Review strategies to improve results on districtwide and statewide tests.

19. Review student guidelines in the student handbook.

20. Review activities and implement new ones with respect to the school mission.

21. Set out the expectations for students and staff in September.

22. Review procedures for parent-teacher conferences and student-led conferences.

Appendix C

Regular Monthly Activities for Principals

> Many administrators admit to being overwhelmed by the workload. Often, this feeling results from a lack of long-range planning. They leave routine tasks until the last minute, then, when one of those day-to-day crises or events happen, they fall further behind, causing themselves more stress. It is crucial to plan time for the important so that you are not consumed by the urgent.
>
> —*Ten Principles for New Principals: A Guide to Positive Action*, M. Joel, p. 20

Check your district's monthly calendar for school administrators. Also, see Chapter 4, "Management Skills," for more time management techniques and tips.

Your regular monthly activities may include the items below. Add to this list as the year goes by:

1. Review your monthly checklist.

   Review multicultural and interfaith calendar for significant dates.

   Set aside time for brainstorming and future planning.

   Identify goals and set priorities for the month.

2. Review budget accounts.

   Compile and submit monthly reports (e.g., attendance).

   Back up electronic records and files.

3. Conduct fire or other emergency drills.

   Meet with custodian; conduct scheduled weekly walk-through of facilities.

4. Review progress toward school improvement plan objectives.

   Review status of school committees.

5. Review and follow up regarding student behavior and discipline trends.

   Review and follow up regarding student achievement statistics.

6. Conduct classroom visits and conferences with teachers.

   Conduct mentoring sessions and induction meetings with beginning teachers and aspiring administrators.

7. Prepare weekly bulletins or updates for staff.

   Draft staff memos.

   Write thank you notes.

   Distribute regular monthly newsletter and calendar.

   Prepare next month's newsletter and calendar.

   Review student newspaper and classroom newsletters.

8. Review school Web page.

   Update office bulletin board.

   Post upcoming events on outdoor display board.

9. Conduct staff meeting.

   Attend team, department, division, grade-level, and school committee meetings.

10. Meet with chair of school advisory group.

    Attend school advisory group meetings.

11. Attend student assemblies and special presentations.

    Support staff and student recognition programs (e.g., student of the month).

    Attend special events: team sports, concerts, etc.

    Observe student council meeting.

12. Attend area and districtwide principals' meetings.

    Attend local professional association meeting.

    Observe district board meeting.

    Visit local service clubs.

Additional Regular Monthly Activities (add your own items here)

-
-
-
-
-

Appendix D

Getting the School Year Started: Checklists for July, August, and September

The following checklists reflect a principal's general schedule. Actual monthly calendars will vary from school to school and from district to district. Many districts have created their own month-by-month calendars and checklists for school administrators. Follow your district's timelines.

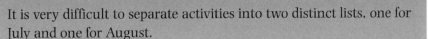

The Summer Months

It is very difficult to separate activities into two distinct lists, one for July and one for August.

In general, you will be finishing off tasks and reviewing progress from the previous year in July, and in August you will be planning and completing tasks for the upcoming school year.

Be sure to take a significant period of time completely away from work to enjoy your holidays.

 JULY

Assuming that you have just arrived at your new school, July is the time to scan the environment.

1. Complete hiring and staffing:

   - Prepare information packages for new staff.

2. Review:

- Scheduling and class lists
- School calendar for coming year
- Collective agreements for all employee groups
- Teacher evaluations
- School statistics, including standardized testing results

3. Review:

- Curriculum and course outlines prepared by staff
- School plans (e.g., coinstructional, staff development, school improvement)
- Letters already sent to incoming kindergarten class and/or Grade 9 class
- Field trip parameters and schedule for coming year
- Fundraising activities

4. Review and revise if not aligned with district policies:

- The district policies and procedures manual
- Student, parent, and staff handbooks

5. Meet with the following people:

- Vice-principal; review and revise administrative responsibilities
- Office administrator; review office routines and responsibilities
- Custodial staff; finalize building goals for coming year
- Local police and fire departments; arrange for school walk-through if appropriate

6. Confirm your membership in educational organizations and professional associations:

- Catch up on your professional reading.
- Develop a personal vision statement.
- Subscribe to and read community newspapers.

> ### August
>
> This is the month to start getting ready for the fall. Prepare now to ensure that support is available when the staff arrives. Cover timetable changes, room assignments, duty schedules, final hiring and anything else that can be thought of and handled in advance. Having these all done ahead of time makes a smooth start for the year.
>
> —*Ten Principles for New Principals:*
> *A Guide to Positive Action*, M. Joel, p. 20

 AUGUST

1. Review entry plan:

   - Establish goals and projects for the new year.

2. Ensure hiring and staffing is complete:

   - Review staff assignments.

   - Finalize master schedule.

   - Review and update individual staff and student timetables.

   - Ensure preparation time is adequate; check all relevant clauses in all collective agreements for all unions.

   - Complete supervision schedules.

3. Review enrollment and class assignments:

   - Make locker assignments.

   - Make room assignments.

   - Review teacher adviser program plan.

   - Update class lists.

   - Distribute class lists and keys to teachers.

   - Ensure school supplies were ordered and have arrived.

4. Review district policies and school procedures:

   - Review procedures for administration of medication to students.

   - Ensure identification badges are ready for new staff.

   - Organize student groups (e.g., bus patrol).

5. Schedule first staff meeting; see collective agreement for direction:

   - Prepare opening remarks and agenda for first staff meeting.

   - Arrange for revised staff handbook to be copied for distribution at first staff meeting.

6. Establish calendar:

   - Establish fire drill schedule.

   - Establish various school committee meeting dates.

   - Check department of education Web site for dates regarding testing and release of results.

   - Check your multicultural and interfaith calendar for significant dates.

   - Review schedule of social activities for students for the year.

   - Enter all pertinent dates on your own calendar.

7. Prepare back-to-school communications for students, staff, and parents:

   - Welcome back letter for staff

   - School opening information package for staff

   - Newsletter and calendar for distribution to students on first day of school

   - Parent newsletter to be distributed during registration process

   - Advertisement for local paper regarding registration details

8. Review transportation plan:

   - Publish information regarding bus schedules.

   - Review information regarding bus routes, drivers, and companies and their contact information, addresses, busing issues, and concerns.

- Drive the bus routes.
- Review attendance boundaries.
- Drive through the school attendance area.

9. Set up meetings with the following people:

   - Vice-principal
   - Office administrator, secretary, or administrative assistant
   - Leaders of programs, divisions, departments, and teams
   - Union stewards
   - Workplace health and safety representative
   - Student leaders
   - School advisory group chair

10. Set up a staff supervision and evaluation plan, in consultation with vice-principal:

    - Conduct new staff orientation sessions.
    - Plan beginning teacher induction program.
    - Prepare orientation program for substitute teachers.

11. Continue your review of school plans; for example:

    - Special education plan
    - Information and Communication Technology Plan
    - School emergency/crisis response plan
    - Communication plan
    - School budget (district and nondistrict funds)

12. Conduct a walk-through with custodian regarding maintenance needs and school readiness:

    - Ensure water lines are flushed.
    - Learn how to operate and override fire alarm and security systems.
    - Become aware of heating system, electrical panels, water shutoff, emergency lighting.
    - Locate health and safety binder.

- Practice using all aspects of PA system.

- Review school hours and bell times.

- Check and test bell signal system.

- Conduct final check of buildings and grounds.

13. Welcome returning staff and students:

- Welcome individual staff members as they return to school.

- Welcome new students and parents as they register.

September

The great thing about each school year is that it gives everyone a chance to renew and to start over with a clean slate. Expectations from parents, students, and staff are high. It is the principal's job to ensure that everyone enters this phase of the year optimistically; just as taking off is the most significant and potentially most dangerous part of an airplane's flight, so is September in the school year's progress. Great caution and care must be taken during September to ensure and maintain a great start.

—Ten Principles for New Principals: A Guide to Positive Action, M. Joel, p. 20

✓ SEPTEMBER

Monthly calendars will vary from school to school and from district to district. Many districts have created their own month-by-month calendars and checklists for principals. Be sure to follow your district's timelines.

In addition to all the regular monthly activities noted in Appendix B, September brings many additional tasks, which are listed below. (Look for items on this list that you can appropriately delegate. See Chapter 4, "Management Skills," for further information regarding the art of delegation.)

1. First Day of School

- Prepare welcome back PA announcement for the first day of school.

- Prepare September update memo to staff.

- Be highly visible.

2. Student Safety

- Collect student medical information and share with appropriate staff.

- Conduct bus safety training for students.

- Ensure placement of safety patrollers and crossing guards.

- Arrange three fire drills before end of first term.

- Review emergency response plans with staff and students.

- Ensure that a safe arrival program (elementary schools) is in place.

- Conduct schoolwide pediculosis check if appropriate.

3. District Reports

- Report daily attendance and enrollment updates to the district office as required.

- Conduct ongoing checks for students who were not present at start of the school year.

- Complete any month-end reports required by the district office.

- Submit proposals for additional district funds and pilot projects.

4. Scheduling

- Reorganize if necessary; make staffing, schedule, and class adjustments as required.

- Follow district procedures and collective agreement provisions.

- Keep staff and parents informed about organizational changes.

- Ensure that teachers submit final class timetables and copies of course outlines.

- Confirm staff coinstructional assignments. (See collective agreement and district policy.)

5. Staff Meetings

- Hold initial staff meeting/regular September staff meeting as per collective agreement.

- Schedule staff meetings and department, grade-level division, and team meetings.

6. School Advisory Group

   - Meet with chair of school advisory group.

   - Hold first school advisory group meeting.

   - Set dates for year's school advisory meetings.

7. Special Education

   - Review special education, ESL/ESOL, and other special programs.

   - Schedule referral meetings for new registrations.

   - Ensure that IEPs are completed.

8. School Plans

   - Update school improvement plan.

   - Update school calendar and student activity calendar.

   - Reconfirm all dates for scheduled standardized testing and release of results.

9. Community Connection

   - Review classroom, grade-level, and department newsletters.

   - Distribute September newsletter and parent handbook.

   - Recruit parent volunteers.

10. Student Orientation

   - Distribute student handbook.

   - Establish assembly schedule, including student orientation.

   - Hold student assemblies regarding code of conduct and other expectations.

11. School and Home

   - Plan for and hold first Open House Evening (Meet the Teacher Night).

   - Hold Grade Nine Parents' Night.

   - Confirm schedule for school photos.

12. Professional Development

- Update staff development plan.

- Plan professional development activities for regular staff meetings. (See collective agreement.)

- Plan for the in-school professional development days if you have any.

- Continue new teacher induction program.

- Conduct class visits daily.

- Set up formal classroom visits schedule. (See collective agreement and district policy.)

- Schedule teacher conferences.

13. Student Field Trips

- Supervise field trip planning and approvals.

- Plan fundraising events for the year.

14. Partnerships

- Re-establish business-education partnerships.

Start your own list of names and contact details for staff at district office (e.g., officers in human resources, transportation, special education, budget services)

Appendix E

Professional Conferences: A List of Web Sites

The Ontario Principals' Council (OPC) does not necessarily endorse the conferences listed below, with the exception of those offered by the OPC. Individuals planning to attend a conference should contact the sponsoring organization to confirm the dates and other details of registration.

AMERICAN CONFERENCES

American Association of School Administrators (AASA)
This professional organization hosts numerous seminars and conferences throughout the year, including a conference especially for women administrators.
www.aasa.org

Association for Supervision and Curriculum Development (ASCD)
ASCD offers a number of regional conferences and workshops and an annual conference. Some regional conferences are held in Canada.
www.ascd.org

International Center for Leadership in Education
The Model Schools Conference is usually held in July.
www.daggett.com

National Association of Elementary School Principals (NAESP)
In addition to an annual conference held in April, NAESP conducts a summer workshop and online training academy.
www.naesp.org

National Association of Secondary School Principals (NASSP)
NASSP hosts an annual conference in February.
www.nasspconvention.org

National Middle School Association (NMSA)
NMSA's Institute for Middle Level Leadership is held each October.
www.nmsa.org

National Staff Development Council (NSDC)
NSDC hosts an annual conference in December.
www.nsdc.org

The Principals' Center at Harvard University
Harvard has an internationally known program of institutes and conferences.
www.gse.harvard.edu/~principals/

CANADIAN CONFERENCES

Canadian Association for the Practical Study of Law in Education (CAPSLE)
An annual conference is presented in the spring in various Canadian cities.
www.capsle.com

Canadian Association of Principals (CAP)
An annual conference is held in May hosted by various provinces in Canada.
www.cdnprincipals.org

Canadian School Boards Association (CSBA)
CSBA organizes an annual conference for school administrators and trustees.
www.cdnsba.org

Ontario Principals' Council
The annual Odyssey Conference is held each November in Toronto.
www.principals.on.ca

TW Branun & Associates
This site lists a variety of conferences and seminars in Canada and internationally. Web casts provide ongoing professional development.
www.twblearn.com

Appendix F

Words of Wisdom:
Advice From Beginning Principals

These words of advice come from first and second year elementary and secondary principals. Their advice has been clustered into 12 categories, which are presented in random order below. Here is what beginning principals said in their own words. Consider how this advice can help you.

1. You're not in this by yourself.

It's wise to ask for advice.

There are people who would love to have you ask their opinions; for example, more experienced colleagues in your district.

Network with your colleagues regularly.

Find a confidant, a mentor. You can't talk to the staff and community about everything. Find someone you can share your doubts with; find a colleague you can talk to in order to make sure you're on track.

Identify resource people you can rely on at the district office and elsewhere.

Work closely with your school administrative assistant or secretary who likely has a wealth of information about the school and the community. Seek their advice; value their expertise; meet with them regularly. Delegate tasks to your administrative assistant as appropriate.

2. You don't have to make decisions this minute.

You need to know when to tell people you'll get back to them after you get further information.

Things are not always as they appear.

Make sure you have all the facts.

3. **Don't try to change everything all at once.**

Respect the history and culture of the school.

Know your community.

Find a couple of key staff members to run ideas by before putting a new model out for general comment from the entire staff.

Do thermometer checks with the staff. Seek feedback.

4. **Don't expect to know all the answers, because you won't.**

Every day brings new experiences.

Constantly re-evaluate your daily priorities.

5. **Have a positive attitude.**

Be enthusiastic. Your mood impacts on the staff.

Don't complain unless you are willing to do something about the situation.

Laugh. Keep your sense of humor.

6. **Keep your focus during negative situations.**

Learn to trust your inner voice and what it tells you about what's right, what's wrong, and what's worth fighting for. Pick your fights carefully.

Know your values. Make decisions with the students in mind and then you'll be able to live with your decisions.

Depersonalize staff reactions to your decisions. Don't let staff issues keep you awake at night.

Unless it's absolutely critical, don't sweat it; most of your worries will never come to fruition.

Deal with human resources issues in a timely manner; don't put them off, or small problems will become big ones.

7. **Remember, it's a team effort.**

Promote teamwork and shared decision-making.

Don't ask for input if you are not going to listen.

Don't forget what it was like to be a teacher.

Hire people with information and communication technology skills.

Acknowledge the good things people do.

Write thank you notes.

Organize and support staff social functions; work together to help a good cause.

Delegate appropriate tasks, even if you do not have an administration team or vice-principal. Match the task with the individual.

Share leadership opportunities.

Enjoy your job and pass that enjoyment along. Cultivate future leaders.

8. **Be visible.**

Try to keep in touch with initiatives in the classrooms, but remember you can't know everything.

Tell staff you want to see students and their work. Welcome students to your office.

You are assuming the office previously held by another person. Does the office reflect you? Do you meet people across a desk, at a round table, in large chairs? Your office sends a message.

9. **Don't be afraid to leave your school.**

Graveyards are full of people who thought they could not be replaced.

Let staff know that generally you will be available either before school or after school, but don't extend both ends of your working day.

Give yourself psychological permission to leave the school when it's appropriate; set a stop time.

10. **Take time for your own professional development.**

Take advantage of professional development activities, especially practical ones specifically related to your new job.

11. **Get ready for the number of hours the job will take.**

You think you know what it will be like to be a principal, but you don't.

It's a job that's never done. Do what's urgent. Have a life. Remember, it's a job.

You can't do it all; you can't get all your work done every day.

No matter what kind of day you have had, when you get home remember that your family and friends are the most important people.

12. **You need to be aware of the perceptions that others have of "the principal."**

    You have a public image; you are always on the job.

    Remember that you work for the district and you represent the district.

    Accept the fact that sometimes you'll feel lonely in your leadership role.

    Know your strengths and your weaknesses, and know where you need help. You're not perfect; don't hide your weaknesses.

    Be real. If your word is good, staff will forgive you an error you've made. If you really care about the kids, parents will support you.

    Live what you believe.

> When you become a principal for the first time, you will face certain issues. One of these is that people will look at you differently, expect different things from you, and hold you accountable in ways that will be markedly different from what they did in the past. Simply stated, you are now "the boss" and this designation carries certain challenges and demands.
>
> —*Beginning the Principalship,*
> J. C. Daresh, p. 107

Appendix G

School Activities and Field Trips

SCHOOL ACTIVITIES AND SPECIAL EVENTS

An Overview

School activities take place during the regular school day as part of the instructional program (e.g., a cultural performance in the gym or auditorium), and outside of school hours as part of the coinstructional program. The coinstructional program is made up of coinstructional activities at the school. The principal should monitor all coinstructional activities.

Traditionally, student activities have included activities such as

- science fairs, public speaking, and debating;
- student government and other student volunteer activities in the school;
- school newspapers and yearbooks;
- intramural sports and interschool athletics;
- arts performances (music, drama, dance);
- service groups and other special interest clubs;
- after-school programs and homework clubs;
- school spirit days and entertainment activities.

Research has shown that student activities, such as those above,

- motivate students,

- develop leadership and other social skills,

- promote positive self-concepts,

- provide a vehicle to create inclusion,

- link academic learning with practical skills,

- stimulate school spirit,

- foster regular attendance,

- recognize students for nonacademic talents.

SOURCE: Adapted from *Principals for Our Changing Schools: The Knowledge and Skill Base*, S. D. Thompson (Ed.), pp. 10-6, 10-7.

School Activities and Field Trips: Getting Started

Review the district's policy and procedures regarding coinstructional activities and field trips. Scrutinize the school's policies and procedures concerning coinstructional activities and field trips to ensure they are in compliance with the district policies and collective agreements. When planning a school activity or field trip involving physical activities, review safety guidelines and safety requirements. Review the previous year's school plan regarding coinstructional activities and field trips.

Recognize staff, students, parents, and community members who contribute to the school's activities and field trip program. Respect the workload and family responsibilities of staff, students, and parents when planning the coinstructional program.

Identify barriers and challenges; for example, access to bus services after school hours, program costs, safety concerns, workload for a small staff, lack of facilities, and attitudes (e.g., beliefs that the coinstructional program robs time from the instructional program). Design creative partnerships among parents, staff, volunteers, and community organizations to help overcome some of the barriers that you may encounter.

Supervision of School Activities

TIPS

The principal of a school shall, except where the principal has arranged otherwise, provide for the supervision of and the conducting of any school activity authorized by the district.

Planning and Organization

In planning a field trip or coinstructional program, consider the following factors:

- Relevant district policies and procedures

- Collective agreement language

- Authorization of the particular activity

- Supervision

- Potential risks, safety and health issues

- The educational value of the activity

- Preventing and reporting injuries

- Transportation

- Budgeting, costs, and fundraising

- Coverage for staff who are out of the classroom or school

- Cultural equity and inclusion

- Recruitment and training of volunteers

- Community partners

- Permission forms and record keeping

- Special needs of participating students (consider students' gender, language, culture, race, ethnicity, religion, sexual orientation, disabilities, etc.)

- Communication and consultation with staff, parents, students, and the school advisory group

- Voluntary nature of coinstructional activities

Fundraising

Many school activities involve some type of fundraising. Ensure that all fundraising activities comply with district policies and procedures; for example, door-to-door canvassing by elementary school students is usually forbidden by the board. Ensure coordination of fundraising activities for the year.

Use appropriate accounting and auditing practices for all fundraising; for example,

- Submit all money raised to the nonpublic school account, following district policy.

- Issue receipts where appropriate or as directed by district policy.

- Follow district procedures for school advisory group and parent fundraising initiatives.

For further information, see the Nondistrict Funds (Nonpublic Funds) section in Chapter 10: "Budget and Resource Management."

Assemblies and Special Events (Daytime)

- Designate a member of the administrative team or seek a staff volunteer to coordinate the assembly and special events program.

- Involve students, the school advisory group, and school clubs in planning, presenting, performing, and evaluating. Teach students about behavior expected in formal large groups; refer to the code of conduct.

- Select a yearly theme or activities that support the school's enrichment program or school improvement plan.

- Post events on the weekly announcements and yearly planning calendar.

- Wherever possible, involve the whole student body or cross-grade and multi-age groups. Invite guests from the community (e.g., a veteran, a local author or artist, a former student, a police officer).

- Use video conferencing to connect students with real-time events.

- Monitor entertainment events and school spirit activities carefully to ensure that they support a positive school climate and have educational value, and that the risk to the health and safety of the students is minimal.

Dances and Special Events (Evenings and Weekends)

1. Adults must supervise all events; one school administrator should always be present at a dance.

- Evening events such as dances, band competitions, and fashion shows may require additional security support. Consider hiring off-duty police officers for school dances. Follow your district's procedures.

- Review school expectations with the supervisors and police officers, and any concerns about the safety of students at the event.

- Expectations for supervision, health and safety, and behavior at a dance or social event that takes place at an off-site location are identical to those for an in-school event.

2. Establish a dress code and ensure student understanding of the code of conduct.

- For dances and other school events, use of alcohol, tobacco, and drugs must be prohibited. Follow district policies and procedures and the code of conduct. Have a plan for how you will respond to infractions.

- When a student or a guest violates the code of conduct, call parents/guardians and arrange for the student to return home. Consider the safety and liability of all concerned when making these arrangements.

3. Establish appropriate procedures for admission to such events to ensure proper supervision and safety.

4. If food is served at the event, recognize that some participants may have food allergies and observe the rules for food safety.

FIELD TRIPS

Preparation

Administrative Essentials

- Follow all district policies and procedures. If you do not find the elements listed below in your district's procedures, consider them when preparing for field trips.

- There are risks for the health and safety of students on all field trips. Some trips, such as a visit to a local museum, may be considered low-risk; others, such as downhill skiing or foreign travel, are considered high-risk events. If you are uncertain about the risks involved, consult the management of the site of the proposed field trip, your superintendent of schools, and another principal whose school has participated in the activity under consideration.

- If an accident occurs on a field trip, follow your district's reporting procedures.

- Review the nature of the trip and any issues related to training, transportation, health, safety, special student needs, costs, and fundraising.

- Visit the site. Teachers or the principal should visit the site (when practical) before the trip to determine learning activities, safety hazards, and special requirements.

- Review the list of participating students with the teacher supervisor in advance.

- Ensure that students with special needs are accommodated. On occasion, it may be appropriate to exclude a student or students. Determine the procedure and criteria for exclusion and publish them well in advance to all participants and parents.

- Provide a list of participating students and information about the date and time of the trip in advance to all staff to facilitate their planning.

- Establish a process for cancellation or postponement, and refund of fees, in case of inclement weather or unexpected events.

- Write thank you notes to supervisors, persons who assisted with the visit at the site, financial sponsors, bus drivers, etc.

Academic Essentials

- Educational outcomes for school activities and field trips must clearly state and support school goals and curriculum implementation. These educational outcomes need to be discussed with the students.

- A representative from the field trip site may visit the school to meet the students, assist with pretrip learning activities, and identify health and safety hazards.

- Pretrip and posttrip assignments should be part of the field trip plan.

- The teacher supervisor should help students develop a set of field trip behavior standards based on the school's code of conduct.

- Evaluate the trip and share results with students, staff, volunteers, the host at the field trip site, and the school advisory group.

Consider attending one or more field trips each year yourself.

TIPS

Authorization

Check district policy to determine the role of the district in the authorization process for field trips, school teams, and athletic events. Consider the following elements when authorizing field trips:

- Written consent from parents or guardians, or the student if he or she is 18 years of age or older, must be obtained.

- Ensure that there is sufficient information on the form for parents to give "informed consent." Use district permission forms.

- Before a major excursion or high-risk trip, a meeting should be held with the parents, students, staff, volunteers, and school administration to review the itinerary, health and safety protocols, criteria for exclusion, standards for behavior, procedures for handling inappropriate behavior, contact information, and any other matters pertinent to the event. Parents should also receive this information in writing.

- Ensure that parents understand that if a student is sent home for inappropriate behavior, it is at their expense.

Supervision

- All supervisors must have appropriate qualifications, and the ratio of students to supervisors must be consistent with the district policy.

- Information about medical needs of students, home and workplace telephone numbers of parents or guardians, etc., must be retained by the supervisor and also at the school.

- A procedure for dealing with a medical emergency while on the trip must be established, including how to cover medical expenses.

- An attendance count should be taken at all points of departure.

- At least one adult supervisor from the school and on-site staff should hold current first aid certificates.

- For overnight trips involving male and female students, the supervisors must be adults of both sexes. Also, supervisors should be sensitive to issues that may arise for students regarding sexual orientation, disability, cultural or religious observances, etc.

- Supervisors should have cell phones, walkie-talkies, first aid kits, and name tags.

- Supervisors should always designate a location to which students must return if they become separated from the group.

Costs

- Field trip and excursion costs should be affordable. Accommodation for students who do not have the funds to participate should be made.

- Funds collected for a field trip or an excursion must be deposited in the school's account and accounted for at the end of the event.

- Money should never be left anywhere other than the school safe or the bank.

- A refund policy for students who cannot attend must be in place.

Transportation

- Prepare a manifest listing the students, volunteers, and staff riding in each vehicle. One copy is to accompany the supervisor of each vehicle and one is to be left at the school before departure.

- Use only district-approved or reputable commercial carriers.

- Volunteers, staff, and students should be discouraged from transporting students in their own vehicles. Check your district policy.

- If district policy permits the use of private vehicles, ensure that there is an adequate number of seat belts for the occupants (including car seats), that the driver has a good driving record, that the vehicle is in good working order, and that both car and driver are adequately insured.

Resources

 TIPS Please see Chapter 28, "Support for School Leaders," for a detailed list of the many resources available when you need help with a specific issue.

The books, Web sites, and journals listed below are presented as a starting point for further reading. Many quality references are available to school leaders, but only a few can be noted here. If you have a favorite resource for principals that is not listed, let us know about it.

BOOKS

Defining the Role and Understanding the Responsibilities

Daresh, J. C. (2001). *Beginning the principalship: A practical guide for school leaders* (2nd ed.). Thousand Oaks, CA: Corwin.

This is a practical guide for the first-year principal or vice-principal, which includes checklists and concise explanations about how to tackle the variety of tasks and to improve skills.

Fullan, M. (1997). *What's worth fighting for in the principalship?* Toronto: Ontario Public School Teachers' Federation; New York: Teachers College Press.

This short volume assists principals with identifying the problems in the school community and deciding if they are worth fighting for. Fullan suggests that principals should "pick their battles" because not all can be won. The author cites examples and gives various solutions.

Fullan, M. (2003). *The moral imperative of school leadership.* Thousand Oaks, CA: Corwin; Toronto: Ontario Principals' Council.

The author challenges all who work in education to rethink the critical role of the principal as school leader in the current era of accountability.

Fullan, M. (2005). *Leadership and sustainability.* Thousand Oaks, CA: Corwin; Toronto: Ontario Principals' Council.

This engaging and powerful book provides clear ideas and strategies for achieving deep, sustainable reform in education.

Komisarjevsky, C., & Komisarjevsky, R. (2000). *Peanut butter and jelly management: Tales from parenthood, lessons for management.* New York: American Management Association.

Although written with business managers in mind, this book uses a parenting metaphor to demonstrate how lessons learned in the family can be applied to managing the workplace.

Lambert, L. (2003). *Leadership capacity for lasting school improvement.* Alexandra, VA: ASCD.

This book provides a comprehensive overview of the steps schools should take to implement the five major prerequisites for high leadership capacity.

McEwan, E. (2003). *Ten traits of highly effective principals: From good to great performance.* Thousand Oaks, CA: Corwin.

In this book the author identifies 10 specific traits and practices of great principals that elevate them above the rest.

National Association of Elementary School Principals. (2001). *Leading learning communities: Standards for what principals should know and be able to do.* Alexandria, VA: Author.

This thoughtful book describes the context for managing schools well. A selective bibliography of print and Web resources rounds out each chapter.

Stevens, L. J. (2001). *An administrative handbook: A view from the elementary principal's desk.* Lanham, MD: The Scarecrow Press.

This handbook offers an overview of the management tasks facing a principal. Although directed at elementary principals, the information will also be of value to administrators in secondary schools.

Whitaker, T. (2003). *What great principals do differently.* Larchmont, NY: Eye on Education.

In this book the author identifies fifteen specific qualities and practices of great principals which elevate them above the rest.

Skill Development

Goleman, D., Boyatzis, R., & McKee, A. (2002). *Primal leadership: Realizing the power of emotional intelligence.* Boston: Harvard Business School Press.

The authors explore the role emotional intelligence plays in becoming an effective leader. They outline six leadership styles and identify the process by which principals can develop EI competencies, motivate staff and students, and foster school improvement.

Ramsey, R. D. (2002). *How to say the right thing every time: Communicating well with students, staff, parents, and the public.* Thousand Oaks, CA: Corwin.

Ramsey has selected time-tested techniques and relevant examples to help principals hone their communication skills.

School Effectiveness and Change Management

Barth, R. L. (2001). *Learning by heart.* San Francisco: Jossey-Bass.

In an engaging, conversational style, Barth looks at practices that truly make a difference for students in schools.

Bluestein, J. (2001). *Creating emotionally safe schools: A guide for educators and parents.* Deerfield Beach, FL: Health Communications.

This award-winning author describes how principals can create a positive school climate while at the same time maintaining high standards for behavior and academic achievement.

Chen, M., & Armstrong, S. (Eds.). (2002). *Edutopia: Success stories for learning in the digital age.* San Francisco: Jossey-Bass.

Edutopia is a collection of useful case studies about topics such as school improvement, student engagement in learning, scheduling, staff development, the role of technology in learning and teaching, and how the change process can transform classrooms and schools.

Dean, S. (2000). *Hearts and minds: A public school miracle.* Toronto, ON: Penguin Books.

An Ontario principal describes how a business partnership leads to school improvement.

Fullan, M. (2001). *The new meaning of educational change* (3rd ed.). Toronto, ON: Irwin.

In this definitive work on the change process, Michael Fullan guides principals through the steps in school improvement.

Fullan, M., & Hargreaves, A. (1996). *What's worth fighting for? Working together for your school* (Rev. ed.). Toronto: Elementary Teachers' Federation of Ontario.

What's Worth Fighting For? presents a realistic picture of the change process and points out the strengths and weaknesses of various models of collaboration and collegiality.

Planning Tools

Barker, C. L., & Searchwell, C. J. (1998). *Writing meaningful teacher evaluations—right now!! The principal's quick-start reference guide.* Thousand Oaks, CA: Corwin.

This guide outlines ways to effectively and efficiently prepare staff performance appraisals and promote staff development. Included is a list of suggested pats on the back and vocabulary. The book is also available on CD-ROM.

Danielson, C. (1996). *Enhancing professional practice: A framework for teaching.* Alexandria, VA: ASCD.

This book provides a framework for teaching and offers guidance for teachers to enhance their practice and for administrators to assess and support their teaching.

Danielson, C., & McGreal, T. L. (2000). *Teacher evaluation to enhance professional practice.* Alexandria, VA: ASCD; Princeton, NJ: ETS.

With concrete examples, useful forms, and assessment tools, this book provides a clear road map to effective teacher evaluation systems that combine quality assurance with professional development for all teachers.

Leithwood, K., Aitken, R., & Jantsi, D. (2000). *Making schools smarter: A system for monitoring school and district progress* (2nd ed.). Thousand Oaks, CA: Corwin.

These Canadian authors describe an ideal, achievable model for assessing a school or board. Included are examples of surveys; information about how to collect, analyze, and interpret information; and an overview of attitudes toward evaluation by staff, trustees, and the public.

Patterson, J. L., Patterson, J., & Collins, L. (2002). *Bouncing back! How your school can succeed in the face of adversity.* Larchmont, NY: Eye on Education.

This book offers concrete strategies and guidelines that work in high adversity, high achieving schools, and procedures to help deal successfully with both ongoing and crisis adversity.

Ross, P. N. (1998). *Arresting violence: A resource guide for schools and their communities.* Toronto: Elementary Teachers' Federation of Ontario.

Ross presents strategies and ideas that work in both elementary and secondary settings.

Senge, P., Cambron-McCabe, N., Lucas, T., Smith, B., Dutton, J., & Kleiner, A. (Eds.). (2002). *Schools that learn: A fifth discipline fieldbook for educators, parents, and everyone who cares about education.* New York: Doubleday.

Featuring articles, case studies, and anecdotes, this book offers advice on organizational learning and staff development.

WEB SITES

Associations

National Association of Secondary School Principals (NASSP)
http://www.nassp.org
Representing 40,000 middle and high school principals, vice-principals, and aspiring principals from the United States and more than 60 other countries, NASSP offers a wide variety of programs and services in areas such as administration, supervision, curriculum planning, and staff development. (This site provides links to all states.)

National Association of Elementary School Principals (NAESP)
http://www.naesp.org
Serving 28,500 elementary and middle school principals worldwide, this site provides membership information, professional development opportunities, and publications.

Educational Resources Information Center (ERIC)

http://www.eric.ed.gov/

The Educational Resources Information Center provides access to resources on educational governance, relationships with the community, supervision of staff, school organization, safety, and improvement.

JOURNALS

The Register. Ontario Principals' Council

180 Dundas St. W., 25th Floor, Toronto, ON M5G 1Z8

Covering a wide variety of topics, *The Register* publishes articles that have a broad appeal. They include advice on legal issues and legislative changes and on practices and programs that are replicable. Opinions in the "One Last Thought" column are a regular feature.

Educational Leadership. Association for Supervision and Curriculum Development

225 N. Washington St., Alexandria, VA 22314

Using a theme format, this well-respected journal selects a wide range of authors from the United States (as well as internationally) to present research-based and timely information. Book reviews, opinion columns, and educational news are featured.

Education Canada. Canadian Education Association

317 Adelaide St. W., Suite 300, Toronto, ON M5V 1P9

This journal covers a wide range of topics of interest to Canadian educators on trends, best practices, leadership, policy development, and research.

Phi Delta Kappan. Phi Delta Kappa

404 N. Union St., PO Box 789, Bloomington, IN 47402

This international organization publishes articles that describe both theory and practice in education. An annual survey of public education in the United States is a feature.

Principal. National Association of Elementary School Principals

1615 Duke St., Alexandria, VA 22314

Of particular interest to elementary and middle school principals, articles cover a range of topics: school organization, school improvement, leadership, special education, technology, staff development, and school safety.

References

Alvy, H. B., & Robbins, P. (1998). *If I only knew.* Thousand Oaks, CA: Corwin.

Anderson, A. (Ed.). (2001). Healthy schools/healthy kids [Special issue]. *Orbit, 31*(4).

Atherton, J. (2002). Entry plan: More than just a checklist. *The Register, 4*(1), 29–31.

Avery, J. (2002). Conducting effective workplace inspections: Identifying hazards that can lead to injury and illness. *The Safe Angle, 4*(1), 3.

Barnett, H. (2001). *Successful K-12 technology planning: Ten essential elements* (ERIC Document Reproduction Service No. ED457858). Retrieved January 11, 2005, from http://www.www.eric.ed.gov

Bennis, W., & Nanus, B. (1985). *Leaders, the strategies for taking charge.* New York: Harper & Row.

Beresford, L. (2002). Do you stop to smell the roses? *The Register, 3*(4), 30–33.

Bluestein, J. (2001). *Creating emotionally safe schools: A guide for educators and parents.* Deerfield Beach, FL: Health Communications.

Brown, A. F. (1998). *Legal handbook for educators.* Toronto, ON: Carswell Thomson.

Brown, G., & Irby, B. J. (1997). *The principal portfolio.* Thousand Oaks, CA: Corwin.

Carroll, D. P. (1999). When reasonable fails: how to deal with parents who harass school administrators. *OPC Register, 2*(1), 24–27.

Charach, A., Pepler, D., & Ziegler, S. (1995). Bullying at school: A Canadian perspective. *Education Canada, 35*, 12–18.

Covey, S. (1989). *The 7 habits of highly effective people.* New York: Simon & Schuster.

Crittendon, R. (2002). *The new manager's starter kit.* New York: AMACOM.

Daly-Lewis, J. (1987). Getting through year one. *Principal, 67*(1), 36–38.

Danielson, C. (1996). *Enhancing professional practice: A framework for teaching.* Alexandria, VA: ASCD.

Danielson, C., & McGreal, T. L. (2000). *Teacher evaluation to enhance professional practice.* Alexandria, VA: ASCD; Princeton, NJ: ETS.

Daresh, J. C. (2001). *Beginning the principalship.* Thousand Oaks, CA: Corwin.

Deschamps, C. (2002). The bottom line: The financial responsibilities of school leaders. *The Register, 4*(1), 17–20.

Dufour, R., & Eaker, R. (1998). *Professional learning communities at work: Best practices for enhancing student achievement.* Bloomington, IN: National Education Service.

Dufour, R., Eaker, R., & Burnette, R. (2002). *Getting started: Reculturing schools to become professional learning communities.* Bloomington, IN: National Education Service.

Fager, J. (1997). *Scheduling alternatives: Options for success.* Portland OR: Northwest Regional Education Laboratory. Retrieved January 11, 2005, from http://www.nwrel.org/request/feb97/article7.html

Fritz, R. (2001). *Think like a manager.* Franklin Lakes, NJ: Career Press.

Fullan, M. (1997). *What's worth fighting for in the principalship?* (2nd ed.). Toronto: Ontario Public School Teachers' Federation; New York: Teachers College Press.

Fullan, M. (2003). *The moral imperative of school leadership.* Thousand Oaks, CA: Corwin; Toronto: Ontario Principals' Council.

Fullan, M. (2005). *Leadership and sustainability.* Thousand Oaks, CA: Corwin; Toronto: Ontario Principals' Council.

Goleman, D. (1995). *Emotional intelligence.* New York: Bantam.

Goleman, D. (1998). What makes a leader? *Harvard Business Review, 71*(6), 93–102.

Goleman, D. (1998). *Working with emotional intelligence.* New York: Bantam.

Grant, C. A., & Zeichner, K. M. (1984). *Preparing for reflective teaching.* Boston: Allyn & Bacon.

Greene, L. E. (Ed.). (2002). Children's heath & safety [Special issue]. *Principal, 81*(5).

Hiraishi, S. (2000). First year magic. *The Register, 2*(4), 30.

Hodgins, L. (2001). Three days of learning: Quick tips and techniques provided to the principal in action. *The Register, 3*(3), 21–24.

Holcomb, E. L. (1999). *Getting excited about data: How to combine people, passion, and proof.* Thousand Oaks, CA: Corwin.

Joel, M. (2002). *Ten principles for new principals: A guide to positive action.* Chicago: Robin Fogarty & Associates.

Johnson, D., & Bartleson, E. (1999). Technological literacy for administrators. *The School Administrator Web Edition, April 1999.* Retrieved January 11, 2005, from http://www.aasa.org/publications

Jukes, I., & McCain, T. (n.d.). *New Schools for the New Age.* Retrieved January 11, 2005, from http://www.tcpd.org/McCain/Handouts.html

Kearns, T., Pickering, C., & Twist, J. (1992). *Managing conflict: A practical guide to conflict resolution for educators.* Toronto: Ontario Secondary Schools Teachers' Federation.

Keel, R. (2004). Managing parental and intruder harassment. *OPC Register, 6*(2), 15–19.

Kuhn, H. W., & Nasar, S. (Eds.). (2001). *The essential John Nash.* Princeton, NJ: Princeton University Press.

More information on bullying: What schools can do. Retrieved January 11, 2005, from http://www.bullybeware.com

National Association of Elementary School Principals. (2001). *Leading learning communities: Standards for what principals should know and be able to do.* Alexandria, VA: Author.

National Association of Secondary School Principals, Developmental Assessment Center. (1998). *Skills for school leaders* [Resource package]. Alexandria, VA: Author.

A national framework for health promoting schools (2000–2003). Sydney: Australian Health Promoting Schools Association. Retrieved January 11, 2005, from http://www.hlth.qut.edu.au/ph/ahpsa

Nelson, B., & Economy, P. (1996). *Managing for dummies.* Foster City, CA: IDG Books.

Newberry, A. J. H. (1996). *A new time—A new schoolhouse leader.* Vancouver, BC: EduServ.

November, A. C. (2001, November). *Managing the transition from paper to light.* Presentation to the OPC Odyssey Conference, Toronto.

November, A. C. (2004). *The scourge of technolust: No more shopping lists!* Retrieved January 11, 2005, from http://www.anovember.com

Peterson, K. D. (1999). Time use flows from school culture: River of values and traditions can nurture or poison staff development. *Journal of Staff Development, 20*(2). Available at http://www.nsdc.org/library/jsd/peterson 202.html

Peterson, K. D., & Deal, T. E. (1998). How leaders influence the culture of schools. *Educational Leadership, 56*(1), 28–30.

Peterson, K. D., & Deal, T. E. (2002). *The shaping of school culture fieldbook.* San Francisco: Jossey-Bass.

Robins, S. L. (2000). *Protecting our students: Executive summary and recommendations.* Toronto: Government of Ontario.

Roder, L., & Pearlman, D. (1989). Starting on the right foot: A blueprint for incoming principals. *NASSP Bulletin, 73*(519), 69–75.

Roher, E. M., & Wormwell, S. A. (2002). *An educator's guide to the role of the principal.* Aurora, ON: Aurora Professional Press.

Ross, P. N. (1998). *Arresting violence: A resource guide for schools and their communities.* Toronto: Elementary Teachers' Federation of Ontario.

Saphier, J., & King, M. (1984). Good seeds grow in strong cultures. *Educational Leadership, 42*(6), 67–74.

Skelly, K. (1996). A letter to newly appointed principals: Ten tips for making the grade. *NASSP Bulletin, 80*(577), 90–96.

Stein, S., & Book, H. (2000). *The EQ edge.* Toronto, ON: Stoddart.

Stevens, L. J. (2001). *An administrative handbook: A view from the elementary principal's desk.* Lanham, MD: The Scarecrow Press.

Straub, J. T. (2000). *The rookie manager.* New York: AMACOM.

Thompson, S. D. (Ed.). (1993). *Principals for our changing schools, knowledge and skill base.* Lancaster, PA: Technomic.

Whitaker, T. (1999). *Dealing with difficult teachers.* Larchmont, NY: Eye on Education.

Whitaker, T., & Fiore, D. (2001). *Dealing with difficult parents (and with parents in difficult situations).* Larchmont, NY: Eye on Education.

Youth homelessness in Thunder Bay: A snap shot. (2001). Thunder Bay, ON: YES Employment Services, Children's Aid Society, Shelter House Thunder Bay. Available at http://www.yes-thunderbay.org/youthhomelessness.htm

Index